T0244783

DYLAN ROBINSON

AGAINST THE ROPES

DEVELOPING GRIT IN THE SPIRITUAL FIGHT

Against the Ropes

Developing Grit in the Spiritual Fight

Dylan Robinson

ISBN (Print Edition): 979-8-35096-775-3

ISBN (eBook Edition): 979-8-35096-776-0

TABLE OF CONTENTS

PREFACE: ARE YOU READY TO FIGHT?

I remember sitting in my Lead Pastor's office in my first ministry season, listening to him tell me about another person who was no longer following Jesus and wouldn't be coming back to church.

"D, why do you think some people keep following Jesus and others don't?"

I thought about it for a second and then responded with one word.

"GRIT."

He smiled, nodded in agreement, and said "Grit, I like that."

I knew I wanted to write a book on Grit one day, so here it is.

Grit: Courage and determination despite difficulty.

In my first book, *Never Going Back*, I shared my life story about how God gave me the power to never go back to my old life. In this book, I want to look at the ability to continue to fight the fight God has called us to, even when it seems too hard to continue to go on.

I want to be very clear before we get started; Jesus is the only reason I am where I am today. If it wasn't for Him, I most likely wouldn't even be on this Earth any longer, or at the very least, behind bars. His grace and mercy changed me from the inside out and I truly am living "Life to the fullest," (John 10:10). With that being said, I had to decide to stay committed to following Jesus even when it wasn't easy. This is where I learned what GRIT was all about. Grit is continuing to press on with your commitment but learning to rely on God's strength and to trust His plans along the way. The day of your salvation and baptism are the highlights (along with so many more things), but to follow Jesus means there's a cost, and we must count that cost before we follow Him (Luke 14:28). Don't misunderstand what I'm saying, following Jesus was the greatest decision I ever made, and He truly saved my life, but it hasn't always been easy.

When you decide to go a different direction than the world, it can feel extremely lonely at first, but you don't find the true meaning in life until you give up your life for Jesus (Luke 9:24). I believe that God allows us to participate with Him on our spiritual journey, and He gives us the freedom to choose to continue to follow Him or not. We see people in Scripture who initially followed Jesus but then decided it wasn't worth it to keep following Him. They ultimately decided that it wasn't worth it, and that it was too hard.

Maybe you're a new Christian and you find yourself overwhelmed by the trials that are still a part of your life, even after following Jesus, and you're not sure what to do. Maybe you've been following Jesus for a long time, and you understand that there are still trials, but perhaps you feel like you're up against someone/something and you've finally met your match, and you feel like you're backed against the ropes. Regardless of what season you find yourself in, this book will help you learn to continue to fight the fight that God has given you. Maybe you're thinking to yourself, 'Fight? What fight? I never signed up for a fight!' After all, doesn't the Bible condemn this type of thinking? Not exactly. In fact, the Apostle Paul often uses metaphors for spiritual warfare as a boxing match throughout his letters, and we'll see how those Scriptures still apply to us today throughout the book.

This is not a book on self-help principles that focuses on pressing on to conquer whatever is in your way, but rather, looking deeper at the fight that we are all in. This is a spiritual fight, and we must learn how to be strengthened by God throughout the fight. With that being said, some trials happen in life simply because we live in a fallen world due to sin (Genesis 3), and we have to learn to develop spiritual grit to endure them.

If you're not familiar with "grit," another word for it is "resilience." Oxford Dictionary defines resilience as "the ability of people or things to recover quickly after something unpleasant, such as shock, injury, etc." In everyday language, this means that when you are knocked down, you get up. When you're pushed back, you press forward. When you are out of options, you create new ones and find a way to move on[1].

Most people love this type of mindset. That's why movies like *Rocky*, *Gladiator*, and *Braveheart* are classics that people love because of the sheer grit displayed. I believe that God has put the desire to fight in every one of us, and if we don't understand what that fight is, then we will end up fighting the wrong fight(s) in life. We will focus our time and energy on things that distract us from the main thing, which is staying committed to what the Word tells us to stand up for, not what culture tells us to stand up for. On top of that, we must avoid the trap of trying to do things with only our own strength because we will always end up feeling overwhelmed and defeated.

We are not capable of fulfilling the plans and purposes that God has for us with our own strength, so we must rely on His power while remaining committed to following Him. Part of our spiritual journey is learning how to rely on God (not ourselves) to develop the resilience to keep going, even when we feel like we can't due to the spiritual attacks as well as the natural trials in life; however, God is faithful, and He's always in our corner telling us what we need to do to keep fighting.

I believe this book will give you insight into the spiritual fight around you as well as give you practical tools to help develop the spiritual grit you need. Are you ready to fight?

INTRODUCTION: AGAINST THE ROPES

"Against the ropes" is an expression used in the boxing world when a fighter has their back against the ropes and has little room to maneuver and escape from their opponent[2]. Typically, a fighter who finds themselves in this situation is in danger of being knocked out because they have taken a multitude of punches that led them to this point. At this point, the fighter must decide in a split second what their next move will be. An inexperienced fighter might be susceptible in this position because they don't have the experience and they might panic and forget the fundamentals they've practiced a thousand times before the fight. This is where they must rely on what they've been taught as well as listen to their corner man (a person who is permitted to be present in a fighter's corner during a boxing match in order to provide advice or assistance to the fighter[3]). You might hear a corner person yelling at them saying things like, "Stay calm, work, and get out of the corner!" On the other hand, an experienced fighter knows not to panic because they've been in that position before and they know how to use the ropes to their advantage.

There's no more famous example of this than arguably the greatest boxer of all time, Muhammad Ali. In October 1974, the famous match called Rumble in the Jungle was one of the most anticipated heavyweight fights between George Foreman and Muhammad Ali. It has been called "arguably the greatest sporting event of the 20th century" and was a major upset, with Ali coming in as a 4–1 underdog against the unbeaten, heavy-hitting Foreman[4]. However, what was more memorable than even the win, was the technique that Ali used to defeat Foreman, which was Ali's introduction of the "rope-a-dope tactic."

The rope-a-dope is a technique where a boxer lays against the ropes while looking for opportunities to counter their opponent. The ropes absorb some of the punch's energy, and this often wears out the opponent[5].

It was from this technique that Ali used Foreman's strength against him, and when Foreman used up all his energy, Ali emphatically won the fight because he learned to keep fighting when he was against the ropes. George Foreman later commented on this fighting technique: "Ali just laid on the rope and I, like a dope, kept punching until I got tired. But he was probably the most smart fighter I've ever gotten into the ring with."

If we're not careful, we can become a dope (stupid) just as George described, when it comes to aimlessly fighting. I'm not trying to be offensive, and I've been a dope many times (as well as sold and smoked dope, so there you go...), but when we lose our composure when we're trying to win a fight (trial) with our own strength, we can wear ourselves out and eventually, lose the fight. There have been many times when I was too aggressive and tried taking matters into my own hands and I ended up doing more harm than good. We need to remind ourselves that Satan is much smarter and more powerful than we are, so we must rely on God's wisdom and strength. If we don't, we will end up losing a battle as a result of the enemy enticing us and making it look like we have him on the rope, but in reality, it was all part of his plan. If we stick to the voice of God (our corner) and rely on our training (spiritual development) then we will end up victorious.

As I said earlier, an inexperienced fighter might not do well in this position because it's a very uncomfortable position to be in. I remember as a kid watching my dad's fights, I would instantly tighten up when he would be against the ropes because I knew it could be a dangerous place for him to be, and sometimes, it was. However, there were other times when he would use the ropes to his advantage by countering with his own punches, using them to lay on to get a breather, and even using them to hang on to his opponent to wear down the other fighter by having to hold up his weight. (By the way, if you're not a boxing fan and I've lost you, then hang on. I promise I won't continue to talk about boxing techniques... as much, that is.)

Even as a kid watching my dad fight, I realized that just because you're against the ropes doesn't mean you're stuck in them! I tell you that story because I feel like it paints a good picture of what can happen when we find ourselves against the ropes in life. You see, just like boxers can at times use the ropes to their advantage, we can use the "ropes" in our lives to our advantage to make us more mature in our faith and strengthen our spiritual resilience. This takes place in a variety of different ways, but we must understand that God uses the trials in our lives (as well as the attacks of the enemy) to strengthen us in our spiritual fight. (James 1:2-3)

Our prayers often consist of us asking God to remove us from our trials (and there's a place for that), but it's through the trials that we develop spiritual endurance (Romans 5:3). A fighter doesn't just show up the day of the fight, put on the gloves and fight. If he/she did this they wouldn't last long at all because a fight has many rounds, and the more rounds the harder it is for the fighter to keep their stamina up. Instead, the fighter spends months training, building up their endurance, and working on their technique so that they are prepared for the day of the fight.

I'm afraid many Christians take the first approach and aren't preparing themselves spiritually for the battle of the day, and they are overwhelmed when the trials in life and the attacks of the enemy come at them. In fact, I've met with many throughout the years who are completely caught off guard when this happens and didn't anticipate the blows whatsoever. How insane would it be if when the fight started, and a fighter got hit they looked at the referee and said, "Why did he do that?!" I know this is an elementary example, and my goal is not to be condescending, but it gets the point across! This is what it sounds like for some Christians, though, much more often than one might think. A trial comes his/her way, and they ask God why He would allow that to happen. Again, it's okay to pray to God and ask Him for wisdom, but we need to know what the Word of God says and then go to prayer and ask Him for the strength to continue through the trial.

There's only one way that muscles can grow and that's from working them out, and while it's not fun at the moment (at first anyway), and it's painful after, eventually we see the results from our hard work, and we begin to enjoy the process more. The Bible supports this when it says, "Now all discipline seems to be painful at the time, yet later it will produce a transformation of character." (Hebrews 12:11 TPT)

FIGHTING SPIRIT

Before becoming a Christian, I had no understanding of the spiritual war going on around me. I just thought I was doing what I wanted to do. There's no such thing as this, though. We are either living for God, or we are against Him (Romans 5:10), and we must decide what side of the fight we are on. Unfortunately, many Christians aren't aware of this, and they have a casual approach to life because, in their opinion, their greatest fight is against anyone who offends them (though we know this isn't true, Ephesians 6:12).

We know from Scripture that we are in a spiritual battle with Satan and his army (Ephesians 6:10-11), and we must learn to combat his attacks in life and continue to fight against him. What does it mean to "fight" in this sense? How do we fight someone we can't see? These were questions I asked myself early on in my Christian walk, but even before I had a theology for it, I knew there was something on the inside telling me that I was born for a fight my entire life. I grew up in a boxing home, so I'm accustomed to this type of language, but I knew that wasn't the fight I was called to. It was something bigger, something more meaningful. It didn't take long for me to realize that the fight I felt called to was the fight for my life, better yet, my soul. When I realized I was in a spiritual fight against a spiritual opponent who comes to "steal, kill, and destroy" (John 10:10), then it all clicked for me!

This is what Paul is referring to in 1 Timothy 6:12 NLT "Fight the good fight for the true faith. Hold tightly to the eternal life to which God has called you."

Paul understood there was a spiritual fight going on and he knew who his opponent was and was not. He not only experienced spiritual warfare, but also an immense number of hardships (2 Corinthians 11), but he knew that he was in the fight he was supposed to be in, which was staying committed to spreading the Gospel. Whether you realize it or not, we are in the same fight that Paul was in, and God wants to strengthen us in our battle to be strong against the enemy (1 Peter 5:8-9) and to spread the Gospel in our daily lives. I know what some of you are thinking, "But I'm not a preacher or church planter like him," and maybe not; however, we are all called to live our lives for Him and use our God-given personality and talents to reach people with the message of salvation that comes only through Jesus.

What does this look like? If you're a hairdresser, then treat every client as if they're someone God sent you to show them His love and care. After all, you have them trapped there, this is a perfect time to share the Gospel because they aren't going to leave until you're done! If you're a teacher, show your students that people care for them and remind them that someone believes in them. If you're a stay-at-home mom, then raise your little ones to grow up to be warriors for God and know you're prepping the next generation. Don't just go to work to do a job (and by the way, I believe Christians should be the hardest working and give their best effort) but believe that God has you there to fight. To clarify, I'm not suggesting you go and punch your boss! Instead, wake up each day prepared to be used by God to share the message of hope with those you meet and believe that God has you there to fight for others spiritually! I'm speaking to believers here, because if you truly believe the Christian message then you believe that those who don't know Jesus are walking around without the hope He offers, and ultimately will spend all of eternity in hell away from Him.

I know some of you are thinking I have a little too much testosterone and I need to chill, but I don't think so. I don't believe that God wants us to spend 1/3 of our lives working[6] just to make money and not use it to further the mission of God. This is how we engage in the spiritual fight every day, by being the light of Christ in the dark world and believing that He will use us to take ground from the enemy by leading others that we encounter to know Christ.

With that being said, we must understand that this doesn't mean there won't be any trials when we join in on God's fight. Jesus assures us there will be trials (John 16:33). As Jesus was preparing to leave His disciples by ascending back to Heaven, He prepared the disciples for what was to come ahead, which were trials that resulted from their faith in Jesus. When we are faithful followers of Jesus, we will be met with various opposition because we are no longer "a part of the world" as Jesus says; therefore, we are considered foreigners to the world. This doesn't mean that we aren't still the same person physically, but we are new, spiritually (2 Corinthians 5:17).

When God clearly changes someone, they begin to talk and act differently because God transformed them into a new person. This is important to understand. When we are speaking about fighting against the enemy, we must understand that the world will oppose us at times because we think differently than it does. While most of us won't ever be persecuted like the early disciples were for their faith, many of us will be challenged by the world and even be told we're being fanatical. Nonsense. We have been saved by the blood of Jesus and we want to give our lives to Him in return, and if others don't understand that then we don't need to "chill out" because we're making them uncomfortable.

Even though Paul lived in a different time, he understood this temptation as much as anyone. Galatians 1:10 NLT says, "Obviously, I'm not trying to win the approval of people, but of God. If pleasing people were my goal, I would not be Christ's servant." If we care more about the approval of others than the approval of God, then we're not fighting the spiritual fight Paul was referring to. I believe the greatest temptation in America (especially the Bible Belt, which is where I live) is cultural Christianity. This is when one wears the label "Christian," but the label has more to do with their family background and upbringing than any personal conviction that Jesus is Lord. Cultural Christianity is more social than spiritual. A cultural Christian identifies with certain aspects of Christianity, such as the good works of Jesus, but rejects the spiritual aspects required to be a biblically defined Christian[7]. Many think they are in a spiritual fight, but really, they are just pretending.

I believe Paul spoke to this when he wrote, "So I run with purpose in every step. I am not just shadow boxing" (1 Corinthians 9:26). Christians must engage in the real fight of Christ rather than going through the motions. Whether you believe it or not, God created you to fight. You can either ignore the fighting spirit He gave you and feel dead on the inside, whether it be materialistic or even something good like social justice (though temporary), or you can put the fighting spirit towards the things that have eternal value, and that's engaging in the work of Christ.

Jesus says, "The harvest is great, but the workers are few. So, pray to the Lord who is in charge of the harvest; ask him to send more workers into his fields" (Matthew 9:37-38). How drastically different would our world look if the church was committed to joining in on the fight that Jesus laid out for us? Are you ready to fight?

I have decided to break this up into three sections to teach you how to keep fighting when you're against the ropes: Faith, Family, Fight.

ROUND 1: FAITH

You must decide to put your FAITH
in God when trials come your way,
or you will never develop the GRIT
you need to stay faithful to Him.

FAITHFUL TO SOMETHING

I will never forget the conversation I had with God after He asked me to leave my current ministry assignment as a youth pastor and plant a church. I told Him, "I don't know what the future holds with this whole church plant endeavor, but I trust you. However, all I ask is that I don't have to get into an *airplane in this next season.*"

I don't know why I felt the need to tell Him that. No one had even talked to me about having to get on one, but I had a suspicion that I was going to have to, and I was terrified. At this point in my life, I had never been on one as an adult and I never remembered going the one time I did when I was a kid.

No exaggeration at all, it wasn't long after this conversation that I got a call from a leader in our denomination telling me that I was going to have to go to a church plant training with several other pastors, and I was going to have to fly. Well, that didn't take long for God to throw my one request away. I mean after all, I was willing to leave my current church (which was known) to plant a church (something that was unknown), so I would have thought He would have answered that one small request.

The group of pastors that I was with discovered that I was a flying newbie, and since I was the youngest one on the trip, they took me under their wings (pun intended) and assured me that everything was fine. Being the youngest on the trip, I tried to pretend that I was fine, but in all reality, I was not fine. When we finally took off and got up in the air, the words of Jesus in the garden of Gethsemane, "My God, why have you forsaken me?" resonated in my ear. Okay, that's extremely dramatic (and probably a little sacrilegious), but I was so annoyed at being in that situation. The next two hours were filled with non-stop turbulence (though I had no idea what that was, I just thought the plane was crashing), lightening, along with the "frequent flyers" looking over at me after every big bump, smiling, and nodding to me, trying to assure me that everything was okay. I thought to myself, 'Well, they are good, so this must be normal.'

When we finally landed, I think I breathed for the first time since we took off and I looked over at them and said, "I don't know how you guys do that all the time, that was crazy." One of the older pastors immediately chimed in and loudly said "I've never been in a plane with it that bad, I thought we weren't going to make it."

That's a memorable experience for me for many reasons, but that trip is one that I look back on and see how God not only got me through my first plane ride, but also allowed me to reflect on how far God has brought me since then as a first-time flier and first-time church planter. Since then, I've been on countless airplanes to go preach somewhere in the country, and I've been able to watch all God has done through the church plant. As a young twenty-three-year-old church planter, I was more concerned with the plane ride than I was about the church plant! This sounds ridiculous, I know, but in my naive mind, I believed that God was going to bless the church, but I wasn't so sure about the pilot flying the plane. I tell that story because I had no idea what the future held for me, but I knew that I had to have faith that God would protect me on the plane as well as the church plant, and He did.

As silly as that might sound to some, I guarantee you that you've had moments where you've had irrational fears about some things, yet not others. (For the record, I was still nervous about planting the church, I just knew I had heard God clearly and I believed He was going to provide what we needed.) Whether you realize it or not, we all put our faith in something or someone. Even atheists do this. Whether it be having faith that your car will safely get you where you need to go, faith that no one will hit you while you're driving, faith that the meal you bought from the restaurant won't make you sick, faith that your doctor properly diagnosed you (by the way, at least one in twenty U.S. adults is impacted by misdiagnosis[8], so let that encourage you) and hundreds of other things that we typically don't stop to think about how much faith is required of those things. Why is it that it can be easy to put your faith in some things, but not others? A lot of this has to do with familiarity because once we've seen it done successfully, we are more likely to have faith in it again.

TESTED FAITH

If we can have faith in the plane/pilot, the car manufacturer, the chef, and the doctor, then why do so many people struggle with their faith in God? The statistics prove that people are struggling with doubt in God more than ever (according to Barna), and this applies to Christians as well. Doubt isn't necessarily a "one-size-fits-all" thing, because some might struggle and doubt the very existence of God, while others have full belief in God's existence, but they doubt that God loves them or has a plan for them. I don't believe doubt is something that God gets mad at us about, but rather uses it as an opportunity to show that we can always put our faith in Him and trust Him in every situation; however, our faith is often tested the most when we are the most uncertain.

We see this in the story of John the Baptist asking if Jesus is the Messiah or if they should continue to look for someone else (Matthew 11:3). Jesus tells us that John is an amazing, Godly man who had been used in a powerful way, but at this moment John was trapped in prison and couldn't see what everyone else was watching Jesus do. I believe there was a part of John that genuinely wanted to make sure that Jesus was in fact the Messiah (though the Spirit already affirmed this to him at Jesus' baptism) so that he could die knowing he did what he needed to do, which was to prepare the way for Jesus. John was in prison and was facing his execution. He probably would have been in a hard place spiritually and emotionally for obvious reasons. Jesus affirms His identity as the Messiah by telling John's disciples what Jesus was doing, but Jesus adds something at the end of the verse for John to hear, "And he added, 'God blesses those who do not fall away because of me'" (Matthew 11:6). I love that it says, "He added." Jesus understood John's question and

He proved He was who He said He was, but Jesus also wanted John (and us) to know that we need to have faith in Him even when our situations don't meet our expectations.

I've watched countless people leave the faith because of their situation not being what they thought it should be, but our faithfulness through the trial proves that our faith is genuine. God understands that we are human and have doubts and questions! With that being said, I do believe the longer we follow Him, He expects us to display more trust in Him and can call us out for our unbelief. We see this with Jesus and the disciples many different times throughout the Gospels. Perhaps one of the most well-known examples of this is when Peter began walking on water.

Matthew 14:24-31 NLT, 24 "Meanwhile, the disciples were in trouble far away from land, for a strong wind had risen, and they were fighting heavy waves. 25 About three o'clock in the morning Jesus came toward them, walking on the water. 26 When the disciples saw him walking on the water, they were terrified.

"In their fear, they cried out, 'It's a ghost!'

27 But Jesus spoke to them at once. 'Don't be afraid,' he said. 'Take courage. I am here!'

"28 Then Peter called to him, 'Lord, if it's really you, tell me to come to you, walking on the water.'

"29 'Yes, come,' Jesus said.

"So, Peter went over the side of the boat and walked on the water toward Jesus. 30 But when he saw the strong wind and the waves, he was terrified and began to sink.

"'Save me, Lord!" he shouted.

"31 Jesus immediately reached out and grabbed him. 'You have so little faith,' Jesus said. 'Why did you doubt me?'"

There are several things I want to point out here, but first, let's point out the fact that Peter was literally walking on water. Not water skiing, but actually walking on water. There's no wonder why this is such a popular story because it's an incredible one! When I first read the story, I felt a little sorry for Peter for getting called out because, after all, he was the only one who got out of the boat. The other disciples stayed back. Jesus calls out his lack of faith and asks him why he would doubt Him. In his defense, this was his first time walking on water, so I think it's safe to say it's understandable for him to begin to panic when he saw the wind and the waves. The longer I study this passage, though, the more I understand Jesus' frustration with Peter.

Jesus had been with His disciples for some time now, and they listened to Him teach about faith, watched Him cure many diseases, cast out evil spirits, and even gave Peter, along with the other disciples, the ability to do the same (Luke 9:6). Right before this miracle, Jesus fed 5,000 men (along with women and children), and there were twelve baskets left over, which was exactly the number of the disciples. This was no coincidence. It was providence. It was Jesus' way of letting His disciples know that if He asks us to do something then we can have full assurance He will provide every time. If you're familiar with this story, it begins with the disciples wanting to send the crowd away into the village to buy food to eat, but Jesus tells them that's not necessary and that they should feed them. Their response is "But we have only five loaves of bread and two fish!" They have a pretty good point! Sure, Jesus had performed miracles and even allowed the disciples to perform some, but this was a BIG deal. However, Jesus performed another amazing miracle yet again.

So, with that in mind, you begin to understand Jesus' frustration with Peter a little more. What I find the most interesting in this passage is how Peter was fine if he kept his eyes on Jesus, but once his eyes got focused on the wind and waves he began to sink. It's been preached and written about many times before, but we need a daily reminder: Keep your eyes on Jesus!

I think Jesus got frustrated because he wanted Peter's trust to increase in Him more because He knew the plans he had for Peter's life in the future. Peter (the rock) was the spokesperson for the disciples often, and even though he had his failures, God used him in a mighty way on the day of Pentecost and helped start the Christian church. Peter didn't know this though, and Jesus wanted him to obey His voice now so that way his faith could be built up for him to grow into the leader God wanted him to be. Like Peter, we never know what God has in store for us in the future, but what we do know is what He's asking from us today. Even though Peter ultimately "failed" the test that day, I believe there was a part of Peter that learned a lot from that experience. After all, he was the only one that got out of the boat! We can be quick to point out his lack of faith, yet many would most likely relate to the other disciples who stayed in the boat.

This story spoke to me as a teenager because I felt like I could relate to Peter (except for the walking on water part, I've never done that). After Jesus radically transformed my life and set me free from a troubled past, I felt like I was the one who stepped out of the boat to follow Jesus. I left the crowd behind me, but there were times that I would get overwhelmed with my new walk with Jesus, but He kept helping me out of the water. Like Peter, I've had many failures, but I've continued to swim back to the boat and have learned to keep my eyes on Jesus more and more each time. As I'm writing this book, I've now followed Jesus for fourteen years, and over time, my faith has developed and I experience less doubt than I did before; however, I've also learned the longer you follow Jesus, the scarier the obedience might seem. Another way to put it is the longer you follow Jesus, the deeper the waters and the stronger the waves get.

Remember what I said at the beginning of this section; we all put our faith in something or someone, but you have to decide whose voice is the most important. The reality is, that it's more dangerous to put our faith in things other than God than it is putting it in Him. Sure, it can be scary surrendering your life to God, but how was life going before that decision? It can be scary giving God your career, but what about wondering if what you are doing is the calling He has for you? It can be scary to give your spouse and kids to God, but how much more stressful is it to wear the weight of the pressure that comes with it? You see when we put our faith in God, it's not burdensome, it's freeing. God has a track record of being faithful, and His faithfulness in the past gives us faith for the future. However, to see God's faithfulness in a situation, we must exercise our faith.

For me, it started with putting my faith in God for salvation, having faith that He would be with my family, faith that He would help me with my call to ministry, faith that I wouldn't die on an airplane going to a ministry event, faith for our church plant, faith for my marriage, faith to be a dad and many other things. The longer I follow Jesus, the more I must look back on and see His faithfulness, but each step requires me to activate my faith. I bet you can relate with my story as well, because Jesus will often call us out of our "boats" to leave the known for the unknown, and this can be scary.

What would you say your boat is? Is Jesus asking you to step out of your boat and have faith that you won't sink in the waves? It's scary to do this, but again, not as scary as not doing it. When God called me to ministry, I knew He wanted me to go to Bible College, but I was scared because I never applied myself in school and I barely graduated from high school. However, I knew he asked me to, and though I was scared to "drown," I knew He would give me the strength and ability to do it. It didn't take long to watch Him give me the wisdom as well as grit to persevere, even though I was learning how to study for the very first time. I was nervous and insecure among my peers, but I knew I had to keep my eyes on Him and know that He had called me to this.

As time went on, I discovered my love for learning, and I began to do well in my classes. As I look back on this time, it's interesting to see where I was then compared to where I am now. I've since finished that degree that I was so scared to get, and as I'm writing this book, I am currently going back to school for higher education. I learned how to apply myself in education little by little, but it all started with getting out of the boat, which was taking my first class.

God put a process in his creation to develop a tolerance (grit) that prepares us for the future and gives us what we need in each season. Every step of the way we have a decision to choose to trust God or not, and He gives us the freedom to choose, but both obedience and disobedience have consequences. Many Christians (and cultural Christians... going back to what I said earlier) would say that they have put their faith in God for salvation, but faith isn't just verbal, it's physical.

James supports this by saying, "'What good is it, dear brothers and sisters, if you say you have faith but don't show it by your actions? Can that kind of faith save anyone?'" (James 2:14). James is not implying that even genuine faith is the basis of salvation; rather, it is the means and instrument by which one is saved[9]. In other words, as we put our faith in God for salvation, we will naturally (or supernaturally) begin to show our faith in God by our actions. So, would you say that you have faith in God? Faith that says, "Jesus, I believe you are my Lord and my savior, as well as the one whom I can have faith in doing what it is you are asking me to do."

NOT SO FAITHFUL

Maybe like Peter when he began to sink, you feel like you've failed Jesus by not trusting Him and you've missed it many times (welcome to the club). That's okay, just decide today to put your faith in God and get back in the fight! As I said earlier in this book, when we realize that we are in a spiritual fight, we no longer view life as choosing to do what we want to do nonchalantly. It's either putting our faith in God or ourselves (which is rooted in evil, Hebrews 3:12). So, we can see that when we put our faith in God initially and continually, it's actually engaging in the spiritual fight that God called us to. The moment we accept God in our hearts and are filled with the Holy Spirit, we are choosing to join God in the spiritual fight against darkness (Colossians 1:1). This is the initial act of faith (saving faith), but then we must grow in our faith (sanctifying faith)[10]. Our faith is meant to grow, not maintain, but if we don't take steps of faith when God asks us to, then it won't grow. Even though Peter lacked faith when he got out of the boat, he undoubtedly remembered it; however, we know that this wasn't his greatest failure.

Peter will always be known as the man who denied Jesus three times on the night Jesus was arrested. Like many of us, Peter thought his faith was stronger than it was. As Jesus is predicting his death and abandonment to His disciples, Peter boldly speaks up and says, "'Even if everyone else deserts you, I will never desert you.'

"Jesus replied, 'I tell you the truth, Peter—this very night, before the rooster crows, you will deny three times that you even know me.'

"'No!' Peter insisted. 'Even if I have to die with you, I will never deny you!' And all the other disciples vowed the same" (Matthew 26:33-35).

I'm sure you know the rest of the story... Peter did in fact deny Jesus three times. Ouch. Jesus predicted that he would do it, but Peter insisted that he was different from the other disciples, but he wasn't. If that was the end of the story then that would be heartbreaking, but it's not.

Jesus had been trying to warn the disciples about what was coming, but they couldn't quite process it. They followed Him everywhere He went and heard everything He said for three years, and Jesus knew His fight on Earth was coming to an "end." He wanted to make sure His disciples were prepared for their fight after His ascension to Heaven, and Jesus knew the darkness was coming for them immediately. Jesus had spent His years with them not to just heal and cast out evil spirits because He could, but to teach the disciples that the Kingdom of Heaven had arrived. Jesus Himself had to grow up in spiritual strength and wisdom (Luke 2:40), so He wanted them to as well. This is important for us to understand! Jesus was fully God, but fully man, and He relied on the Holy Spirit to make Him strong (Philippians 2:7).

Jesus didn't begin His ministry until He was thirty years old because God had not called Him to begin the ministry yet and was still preparing Him. Once Jesus began His ministry, the Spirit led Him to the desert to be tested by the devil for forty days while He was fasting. Doesn't this seem odd to you at first? Jesus, the Son of God, begins His ministry by being led to the desert to be tempted by the devil. I'm not going to do a deep dive into this here (though you should sometime), but Jesus was learning how to rely on the Spirit in the midst of temptation. Scripture teaches that Jesus was tempted as we were (Hebrews 14:15) but didn't sin. "Well, He was God...", yes, but remember, He gave up His power and instead taught us how to rely on the Spirit.

This is the epitome of spiritual grit! So, once He gathered His disciples and began teaching them about how to rely on God, it was because He was teaching them from first-hand experience, and He knew He wouldn't always be around, so they needed to learn His ways. This is why Jesus showed frustration in the garden of Gethsemane when He asked Peter, James, and John with Him to pray before He would be crucified. Jesus was back in a vulnerable state (just like at the beginning of His ministry in the desert), but this was worse because it was the end of His ministry. He's overwhelmed to the point that He begins to sweat drops of blood (Luke 22:44), and when He needs His inner circle the most, they let Him down by sleeping.

"40 Then he returned to the disciples and found them asleep. He said to Peter, 'Couldn't you watch with me even one hour? 41 Keep watch and pray, so that you will not give in to temptation. For the spirit is willing, but the body is weak!'" (Matthew 26:40-41).

Jesus needed their support because He knew what was before Him, but He also needed them to know darkness was coming for them. I'm sure as they woke up (the third time) they were asking themselves, "What's the big deal, Jesus? We're tired and we just needed a little nap." Little did they know (even though Jesus was trying to warn them) that in just a few moments, Jesus would be betrayed by one of His disciples, Judas. During the Last Supper, Jesus realized what was about to happen, and He understood that it was Satan at work.

"As soon as Judas took the bread, Satan entered into him. So Jesus told him, 'What you are about to do, do quickly'" (13:27 NIV).

Jesus didn't see Judas' betrayal just as him being a sell-out, but rather as evil. That's why Jesus was adamant that the other disciples needed to be awake, not just physically, but spiritually, because there was a war going on that they didn't even realize. Once the war began, they weren't prepared, and they all deserted Him (Mark 14:50).

Let's go back to the words of Peter, "I will never deny you." Again, Jesus knew Peter would deny Him (as well as Judas) but look at what Jesus told Peter right before this.

31 "'Simon, Simon, Satan has asked to sift each of you like wheat.

32 But I have pleaded in prayer for you, Simon, that your faith should not fail. So, when you have repented and turned to me again, strengthen your brothers."' (Luke 22:31-32)

Notice how Jesus calls Peter by his old name, "Simon." He calls him this perhaps to help him understand that he's overly confident in himself and is not being who Jesus needs Him to be. On top of that, I want to point out that Jesus says Satan asked to "sift" him as well as the other disciples, but Jesus intercedes for them. Jesus then acknowledges that Peter will fail but knows Peter will repent, and then afterward he needs to go strengthen his brothers. So, when Jesus called out Peter, James, and John for sleeping, He knew what was at stake and what would eventually happen, which was that all the disciples would desert Him when he was arrested and awaiting His crucifixion. Jesus knew the fight had begun.

As the story goes, Jesus eventually was killed, and Satan thought he had won. Meanwhile, Peter and the disciples experienced heartbreak as their friend and teacher died, and they didn't have the faith to stay with Him until the end. However, we know that's not the end of the story. Jesus rises from the dead and gives Satan and hell the ultimate counterpunch and destroys the power of sin for those who put their faith in Him. This is amazing news for the disciples, but they are reminded that they weren't faithful to Jesus when He needed them, but Jesus knows this isn't the end for them, just the beginning. Jesus restores the disciples and even addresses the issue with Peter one-on-one and encourages him to continue to follow Him, even after denying Him. Peter learned from this, and his faith continued to grow, and after Jesus ascended into Heaven, He poured His Spirit out and Peter preached the first sermon that led to the beginning of church.

Let me point out the obvious, we will never be in the (literal) same spot as Peter, but I do believe there's a parallel there that we can all relate to. Has there ever been a time in your walk that you were like Peter in this situation? You thought you had more faith than what you really did? You were sure you wouldn't be influenced by others (it was the guards for Peter), but you were? This is a humiliating place to be, and we're embarrassed that our faith wasn't stronger; however, just like Peter, Jesus isn't done with us either! When we find ourselves in this place, we must decide what we will do next. Who/what will we put our faith in now? Where will we go? Are we done with Jesus because we failed Him? Have we decided to stop going to church because we will see people who know what we've done?

Peter had to get over this to do what Jesus still had for him to do. When he got up to preach (now filled with the Spirit), there most likely, were people who witnessed his denial of Jesus, but he didn't let that stop him from preaching. Guilt and shame are tactics of the enemy, and he uses these things to try to prevent us from doing what we feel God is leading us to do. Satan thought he won when he got Judas, one of Jesus' own disciples to betray him, and got Peter to deny Him, but Peter used this against him. This is what it looks like to use the ropes to our advantage! The thing that we're ashamed about can be the thing that God can use to shame the enemy! Peter's failure didn't disqualify him but rather validated the message that he preached.

Just as he called the people he was preaching to, "repent of their sins and receive the forgiveness of Jesus" (Acts 2:38), he too did the same thing. This must have made Satan furious! As the Spirit began to use him and the disciples in powerful ways, the words of Jesus undoubtedly ran through his mind, and he began to understand what Jesus meant during the times He was preparing Peter for what was to come. I'm sure he and the others laughed at the time he started to drown when he walked towards Jesus or when they didn't know where they were going to get the bread from. I'm sure he even reflected on the time he denied Jesus the night He was arrested and possibly grinned at how far he had come. Peter made a recommitment to put his faith in Jesus and he did until he was eventually martyred for his faith. As much as anyone, Peter knew that we were in a spiritual fight, and he knew we had to have faith in Jesus initially, but also continuously. It makes sense why he would write the verse below:

"Like newborn babies, you must crave pure spiritual milk so that you will grow into a full experience of salvation" (1 Peter 2:2).

Jesus knew that "Simon" needed to grow into "Peter," and this was a long process filled with many "failures." However, Jesus used these failures as things to mature his faith and become the leader that we read about beginning at Pentecost. Don't let your failures prevent you from being faithful in the future.

FAITH AFTER FAILURE

Though I'm known (in my circle) for being radically changed and never going back to my old life, I want to be crystal clear: I fell into temptation time and time again after being saved. I know that's an obvious statement if you've been a Christian for some time because you know that just because we're saved doesn't mean we're perfect, but failure was hard for me after becoming a Christian. I knew that I didn't save myself and I had proper theology regarding salvation (grace through faith), but it was deeper than that. I so desperately wanted to live for God, and I didn't want to sin against Him in any way, but I'm human and I did. Sure, it wasn't the public sin that was as obvious as others, and it wasn't the sin that I once was known for, but it was still a sin.

When I fell into sin, I would confess and repent to God and ask Him for forgiveness and He would (and still does) kindly extend it to me, but the guilt and shame would stay there for a while. Being a new Christian, I just assumed that this was my punishment from God for sinning. I would begin to tell myself that God didn't love me, and He was probably done with me, and I blew it. Random thoughts would come into my head, telling me that I might as well give up and go back to my old lifestyle since I messed up, again. I was so new to my faith that I wasn't grounded enough to discern the lies of Satan from the truth of God, so I wasn't able to know this wasn't true.

I had people around me to help me, but I didn't want to open up because I didn't want them to look down on me and think I wasn't the real deal. So instead, I kept to myself and took these lies "on the chin" and beat myself up until some time had passed. I repeated this pattern until I found myself sobbing and telling God I was sorry for letting Him down again, and I understood if He didn't want me any longer.

I will never forget that day, because, in that moment of me saying that and crying out to Him, I felt the love of God in a way that assured me He still loved me and wasn't going anywhere. He reminded me that this is why He sent His Son Jesus to the Earth, to cover the price for my sins, not just the old ones, but the current ones as well. This led to more sobbing and eventually a big smile on my face! I understood that Jesus died to cover my sins, but I bought into the lie that it was only for the sins of my past. I know that some seasoned Christians are thinking that this is a discipleship issue, but it wasn't that I hadn't heard this before, but I didn't believe it to be true for me because of my own dysfunctional relationship with my earthly Father.

It was at that moment that I realized the relationship aspect of my faith. I had to see God as my perfect Heavenly Father, not as some far-off deity in the sky who was always disappointed with me. This changed everything for me, and it even changed my approach to the way I fought temptation. Satan would overpower me time and time, again by relying on my own strength and then beating me up and lying to me after I was down, and he tried to get me to give up on my faith in God. When I started listening to God (who was in my corner), I was able to keep going when I was against the ropes when temptation was up against me and I found myself becoming more and more victorious, and He was there to pick me up even when I found myself knocked down again.

During this season of being a young Christian, I learned that God would give me the love and strength that I needed, but I also learned that there was something that only I could do for myself, and that was to not lose faith. God will provide the rest for us as we partner with Him on this spiritual fight, but the one thing He can't do for us is give us faith. Through the years, people have kindly told me that they were impressed with my ability to keep going in my faith amidst adversity (spiritual grit), but in hindsight, maybe it wasn't that I had so much grit as much as it was that I had faith.

We need to continue to grow in our faith, and no matter how many times you've begun to drown, tried to figure out how to solve a problem that was too big for you (feeding the 5,000), or even denied Jesus, He is not done with you! Hopefully, you're more convinced than ever that you're in a spiritual fight, and hopefully, you see that God has been developing your spiritual grit all along. When life has you against the ropes, your faith will be tested, and you must decide to keep going or to throw in the towel. Keep fighting by putting your faith in Him and be faithful to the call He's put on your life.

GROWN UP FAITH

The longer we follow Jesus, the stronger our faith should get. In any relation-ship, the more you're around someone, the more you can see if you trust them or not. In the same way, the longer we're around God, the more we realize we can trust Him in everything. This doesn't mean no questions remain after we believe in Him for something and yet we don't see anything happen, but we can trust that His plans are good, and we have faith that His ways are better. This doesn't mean that we lose hope for God to bring healing or provision to a situation, in fact, we need more faith for these things! Instead, we have full confidence that God is willing and able to move in any situation where we pray for His power to be displayed, but if the result doesn't end up looking like we had hoped, then we trust His plans anyway.

There have been times in my life when I have watched God answer some incredible prayers, such as the salvation of others, physical healing, financial provision, divine appointments, supernatural peace in hard situa-tions, and many other things. At the same time, there have been many times that I thought that God was going to answer my prayer differently than He did. When I find myself in these situations, my faith is tested. Do I still believe that God is good? Do I still believe that He is just? Do I still believe that He can answer prayers? My answer is still yes.

I have prayed for the salvation of some of my family members since the moment I got saved, and while I've seen some breakthroughs at times, I would be lying to say that the situation looks like I thought it would. There have been many times when I've felt discouraged and wondered if they were ever going to get saved, and even times when I didn't feel like praying for them any longer. This is when my faith is stretched and my spiritual grit is strengthened, though. As I continue to read the Word of God and pray to Him and give Him my burdens, I experience His peace and I continue to believe that He's still working on the situation. I must understand that there's a spiritual battle going on in their lives as well, and while God is more powerful than the enemy, He also gives everyone free will to decide what to do. So, I continue to pray that God will reveal Himself to them in a powerful way and ask for Him to protect them from the enemy's plans for their lives. Don't stop praying and believing in a miracle for them.

Too many Christians walk around defeated because God hasn't answered their prayers yet, and they live with constant discouragement, but that's not what God desires for us. Look at what Paul writes about God's peace:

"Don't worry about anything; instead, pray about everything. Tell God what you need and thank him for all he has done. Then you will experience God's peace, which exceeds anything we can understand. His peace will guard your hearts and minds as you live in Christ Jesus" (Philippians 4:6-7 NLT).

How can one not worry about anything? By praying to God and thanking Him for what He's already done. When we remember God's track record of being faithful, we can have peace knowing He'll be faithful again. This may seem outrageous, but not as crazy as thinking your worry is going to change anything. This is why Jesus constantly reminded people to not worry and to believe in God's provision for them. If you never grow up in your faith in this area, then you will never grow in your faith, and you won't experience God's peace.

It's been said, "know God, know peace, no God, no peace." Some Christians have been saved for a long time, but their faith is one of a baby Christian. They've never graduated from the basic teachings of Jesus, and they don't develop more trust. This is why the author of Hebrews says, "So let us stop going over the basic teachings about Christ again and again. Let us go on instead and become mature in our understanding" (Hebrews 6:1). We must grow in our faith so that when things happen to us that we don't like, then we can still have peace. If we're going to grow in our spiritual grit, then we're going to have to grow in our faith. Then, as we grow in our faith, the enemy knows we're not as weak as we used to be.

FAITH REFINED

I'm completely deaf in my right ear. It wasn't always like this though.

When I was twelve years old, I woke up one morning and fell right back down. I tried to stand back up and I fell right back down again. I was at my grandmother's house, so I yelled out for her because I was confused about what was going on. Once I explained the situation to her, she told me it was my equilibrium that was off. I had no idea what she meant by that, but I just knew that I had a baseball game to attend that night and I was pitching, so I just needed her to fix it quick. As the day went on, I was able to stand up fine without any issues and went on to pitch a perfect game that night (okay, that was a lie).

A few weeks went by, and I hadn't had any issues since that morning until I woke up again, and this time, I couldn't hear in my right ear. This freaked me out, to say the least. I was with my grandma again (see the trend?), and this time I yelled out louder than the first time.

"I can't hear in my right ear!"

We tried every home remedy that we could try, even the strange wax candle that you put in your ear and catch on fire! Nothing worked. My cousin began messing with me because he didn't believe I couldn't hear, so every few minutes, I would look over and find him whispering in my ear without me knowing. This made me mad and scared all at the same time. I was freaking out, but I didn't want to act scared, so I stopped talking about it and went on with my life for a few days.

Then, one day, I woke up in the middle of the night feeling like my head was about to explode. I had never felt pain like this before and it was at that moment that I knew something was seriously wrong. I woke my dad up and explained to him what was wrong and to his surprise, I still couldn't hear in my ear and now I had a terrible headache. He took me to the emergency room and from there, we discovered I had a tumor in my inner ear, which was causing the hearing loss and pain. I had no idea what was ahead, and I was nervous, though I pretended to be fine. After consulting with one of the doctors who specialized in this type of thing, I discovered that I was the youngest person in the world at that time to have this happen. I'm not sure if they thought I would think this was cool or not, but I wasn't impressed. I just wanted to know if I would be able to hear or not. The doctor explained to me that they were going to have to cut into my ear and remove the tumor without any issues to my brain, even though the tumor was very close to it. That's great, but I just wanted to know if I would be able to hear again.

That's when he kindly said, "Unfortunately not."

After being so "tough" through this whole process, I finally broke when I heard that news. I began to cry in the doctor's office and my family came around me and comforted me. I was heartbroken because I had high hopes that I was going to be able to hear after the surgery, but now, that was no longer a possibility.

As time went on, I adjusted to not being able to hear, and even though I didn't have a relationship with God, I found myself grateful that I had one good ear still. I started noticing people who were less fortunate than me who couldn't hear at all, couldn't walk, see, or talk very well. The more I looked around, the more I realized how fortunate I truly was. It's not that I wasn't aware of these situations before, but I hadn't ever thought too much about it because I was so focused on my well-being. My situation was (and is) unfortunate, but it has made me grateful for the things that I do have.

I don't believe that God caused my tumor, but He did allow it. Even before I was a Christian, it made me a more grateful person. I had a decision; do I feel sorry for myself, or do I get back up and be more grateful for all that I do have? If that tumor was just an inch closer to my brain, then my whole life would have been drastically different, and being deaf in one ear would have been the least of my worries. This is what can happen to us when we personally go through trials. We can become more aware of the needs around us as well as be more grateful for the things that we do have rather than just focusing on what we don't have.

I remember the day after this major surgery, I had to walk around the halls, but the nurses warned me that I had to take it slow and that there would be a lot of pain and it might take me a while to find my balance again since I no longer had an inner ear. Even as a twelve-year-old, I took that as a challenge to beat the odds. I was determined to walk around that hospital as fast as I could and as many times as I could, and I did.

"Woah, slow down!" they said. "Take it slow."

If I wasn't going to be able to hear, then I was determined to show them this wasn't going to stop me from moving on. Each lap around the hospital was an incentive to keep going because the more I walked, the faster I got to leave. They weren't kidding though, it hurt terribly. I eventually got to go home, and I had to learn how to live with my new situation. I eventually adjusted and now I can't remember what it was like to be able to hear out of both ears.

I say that whole story to get to this point: This trial in my life taught me gratitude and humility.

Again, before I was even a Christian, losing my hearing made me more thankful for the many blessings that I have compared to others. Once becoming a Christian, this gratitude has grown even more. In fact, I take it as a compliment when people are surprised to discover I can't hear. As much as I wish I could hear out of my ear again, I'm thankful that I have one that works. Not only did it make me grateful, but it also humbled me. Though I learned to adjust with only one ear, it was humbling at times (and still is) when people are talking to you, and you don't even know it. I know that seems dramatic, but it's true. This experience has taught me a lot.

Some of you might be thinking that this is a small problem compared to what you're facing physically (or any other way), and it probably is! However, my point is that the trials that we go through are things that can shape us into who God desires us to be. Not that He causes them (though He can), but He uses them to help us grow up in our faith.

Too many Christians are ungrateful because they feel like they don't have what they think they deserve, rather than being grateful for what they do have. It's easy to become entitled to things, and we forget how blessed we really are. Some would love to have our problems, and if we notice how blessed we are then we will regain an appreciation for the many blessings that we do have. No matter what you think would drastically improve your life if you got it, I can assure you that you will eventually become focused on something else that you don't have if you're not content with your current situation. That's why someone like Paul who went through so much can say something like this:

"11 Not that I was ever in need, for I have learned how to be content with whatever I have. 12 I know how to live on almost nothing or with everything. I have learned the secret of living in every situation, whether it is with a full stomach or empty, with plenty or little. 13 For I can do everything through Christ, who gives me strength" (Philippians 4:11-13 NLT).

Most people (even non-believers) are familiar with that last verse: "For I can do everything through Christ, who gives me strength." It sounds exciting, and that's why many athletes write it on their faces or people get tattoos of it because it makes us feel like we can accomplish anything, and they're right. We can when God's in it; however, Paul isn't talking about accomplishing things by our might. He's not talking about the ability to keep going in the spiritual fight when our backs are against the ropes with willpower, but by contentment.

What? That's not very exciting. I like the version of Tim Tebow going out with it on his face and running over the defense. Paul knew he could do "everything" because he trusted in God's strength, which allowed Him to be content in every situation. He knew that if God was with him, then no matter how bad it may appear on the outside, he could rest knowing God would provide everything He needed. This didn't mean that he didn't have trials and it didn't mean that he loved going through them, but He trusted that God would get Him through.

Not only did Paul learn to be content (grateful) in hard times, but He was also humbled through them. God used Paul unlike any of the other disciples as an instrument to tell people throughout the world about Jesus. He even received Heavenly revelations, so there was a temptation for him to become proud just like any of us. God used trials to help him in this area.

"So, to keep me from becoming proud, I was given a thorn in my flesh, a messenger from Satan to torment me and keep me from becoming proud" (2 Corinthians 12:7 NLT).

In this case, God did cause a trial to take place in his life. There are times when God places us in a specific trial so that we will stay humble and continue to grow in our faith. For Paul, he recognized this trial as something that was used for his own good. We don't know exactly what this "thorn" is, but what we do know is that it was something that tormented him. Torment is a very strong word that suggests suffering. This wasn't some small situation that he could easily ignore. It was very crippling to Paul, and he faced limitations on the daily. Rather than getting bitter at God and giving up, he saw this as a time to have gratitude and humility and he was content with it.

If you're like I was when I first read this Scripture, you're probably wondering why he didn't pray for it to go away? He did.

"8 Three different times I begged the Lord to take it away. 9 Each time he said, 'My grace is all you need. My power works best in weakness.' So now I am glad to boast about my weaknesses so that the power of Christ can work through me. 10 That's why I take pleasure in my weaknesses, and in the insults, hardships, persecutions, and troubles that I suffer for Christ. For when I am weak, then I am strong" (2 Corinthians 12:8-10 NLT).

Paul begged (again, strong language) for God to take it away, but He didn't. In fact, God told him that it was given to him to keep him from being proud, and Paul knew this was God's will for him, so he stopped praying for it to be taken away.

There are times when God wants us to continue to pray for healing and breakthroughs (James 5), but there are also times like this when God tells us that it's His desire for it to happen. This might be a hard pill for some of us to swallow, but when we're content with God, then we can rejoice and trust Him. Paul was used to healing countless people, yet he wasn't healed from his own limitations. Rather than limiting God's reputation, it built it up! Think about it. If Paul could heal with his own strength, then he would certainly use his power to heal himself, but if it's God's strength through Paul, then God chose when to heal and when not to, which would prove Paul's power came from God, not himself. So, Paul remained grateful, stayed humble, and God used him to do mighty things. It's obvious that Paul was just glad to be used by God rather than be healed. Rather than allowing it to hinder his witness, Paul allowed it to be used to boast about his weakness and be an example of God's strength.

You might be going through something that seems to limit you, but rather than counting it as a weakness, view it as a strength. When God uses us in our weakness, it's easier for Him to pour out His favor on you because it's obvious that He's the one being glorified, not you. Perhaps you've been given a limitation as something that God wants to use to reach others. Maybe some would never put their faith in God if it wasn't for them seeing God's strength in their own life. Not that our weaknesses are what we get our identity in, but rather people see our faith is strong in God despite our inability. God will use anything to make us grateful and humble, and it's not our job to know why we're going through something. We just need to trust Him in the process.

Earlier, I mentioned my ear was something that has kept me humble, but this was only the beginning. As I became a Christian, I answered the call of ministry and I was terrified (for many reasons), but one of the main ones was that I couldn't speak well, and I didn't think I was smart enough. As I obeyed God, He gave me the ability to speak as well as understand the Scriptures in a way that I never thought I could. He wasn't worried about my inability; He just wanted me to put my faith in Him and give him my availability. As I put my faith in Him, He proved Himself to be faithful to me. For me to preach around the country, be a church planter, graduate from college, and write books is so outside my ability you can't even imagine (unless you used to know me, then you can). As God has used me in ways I never dreamed of Him using me, I must continue to fight the urge to become ungrateful and proud, and He still uses my weaknesses to help me. We can't forget that it's only by God's grace that He saved us and is using us, and we need to stay faithful to Him whether we're being encouraged or refined.

GOD-SIZED FAITH

Since becoming a Christian, I've had many people tell me that they believe God is going to heal my ear. I was weirded out by these statements as a new believer, and I would sarcastically think, "God would need to supernaturally grow my inner ear back then."

I didn't say this out loud, but I wanted to. The more familiar I became with it, the more I realized how many miracles there are in both the Old and New Testaments. Being a new Christian, I would read the commentaries in my study Bible, and I would wonder how these commentators would explain the different miracles. More times than not, they would talk about how Jesus' power proved He was from Heaven and would then apply the miracles to our own situations. The thing I didn't read much about was how we too should expect to see miracles. I never heard about miracles being talked about and I didn't hear many sermons about believing for God's miracles, so I sort of ignored it and just assumed that God didn't do miracles any longer, or at least not "big ones."

Once I graduated high school (which was a miracle in itself), I wrestled with where I was supposed to go to school. I was getting discouraged because it seemed like everyone else knew where they were going to school and what they were going to do, but not me. "God, I need a miracle!"

I began to hear about this local Christian college that was a part of a different denomination than I was affiliated with, so I didn't think much about it. As time went on, I kept hearing about it almost everywhere I went. I heard it on the radio, I saw it on social media, and heard random people talking about it, and then one of my friend's mom approached me and said she felt like I was supposed to go to this school. Okay, God, you have my attention.

After eventually giving in, I moved into my dorm and set off on a brand-new adventure, and I was scared out of my mind. How was I going to be able to graduate college if I could barely graduate high school? I hadn't studied for a test in my life up to this point, but I just continued putting my faith in God and trusted that He would help me.

The school traveled to a campground to have a spiritual retreat before kicking off the year. As soon as we got to the campground, I immediately began to question God on why He had sent me there and wondered if I had heard Him wrong. I wanted to leave and move back home, but little did I know that God had me right where He wanted me. On our final night there, I was still in a bad mood and was sure that God had "missed" this one. The speaker that night had us get away by ourselves and begin to pray to God and seek Him going into the school year. He told us if we had any questions or doubts, to let God know by writing them down and to trust that He would answer.

"Great idea," I thought. I would love to tell God how much He messed up sending me here out in the middle of nowhere with all of these "strange" people. As I opened my journal and began to write, the first thing I jotted down was, "GOD, I NEED CONFIRMATION! I need to know that I am called to be here. I need to know that you called me to the ministry. I need to know that you have a plan for my life." Honestly speaking, I was a little sarcastic because I was so frustrated with the situation.

As I got done writing my pathetic "poor me" speech, a classmate of mine began to pace back and forth in front of me. Annoyed, I looked at him and gave him a look that implied, "What are you doing walking back and forth in front of me like a crazy person?"

I had just met him that day and briefly talked to him about my life and explained to him my family situation, so he hardly knew me at all. Suddenly, he stopped pacing back and forth and looked at me in a very stern way to the point that it freaked me out a little bit because I knew he was a timid person. He said something to me that forever changed my life: "God told me to tell you that you need confirmation. He's called you to be here. He's going to use you and your story to impact people's lives, and he placed your God-family for a reason." He told me many more things he shouldn't have known. As you can imagine, I froze and began to weep.

I didn't know this guy at all, but I knew that God just used him to affirm me in a way that I had never been affirmed before. I couldn't believe what had just happened; God just answered my sarcastic prayer because He's so good and He loves us so much! After the service was over, I ran up to my classmate and asked him to retell me some of the things that God had told him to tell me, but he had no recollection of them.

I said, "What do you mean you don't remember?! You just told me, so tell me again!"

He responded, "I don't know what I said because they weren't my words, they were God's. I just know that I was supposed to tell you that."

I walked to my cabin and laid my head on my pillow that night knowing that God was watching over me and had me right where He wanted me.

I will never forget that moment until the day that I die, because I knew that it was a miracle. Maybe it wasn't God splitting the Red Sea, but it was enough for me to realize God had heard my passionate prayer. When my friend said the word "confirmation," I immediately knew that this was straight from God, because that's the word I prayed over and over without anyone hearing me. At that moment, I knew that God still did miracles, and I had just seen one and no one could take that from me.

Since then, I've watched God do something like this numerous times. He gives words of knowledge for someone and it "just so happens" to be the thing that someone needs to hear. I've watched Him provide financially in ways that make no sense whatsoever, other than the fact that God provided (to the dollar amount at times). I've watched Him save the "unsavable," restore families, and heal people emotionally and even physically. I still believe that God is a God of miracles! I think we are too quick to forget the miracles that God has already performed time and time again. Sure, they might not make the headlines, but you know that there's no other explanation than God intervening.

At the same time, there are many situations that I've prayed for, believing for a miracle and I never saw one (or haven't yet). Not going to lie, I'm not sure why this happens, and there are times that I've been discouraged by the lack of apparent activity, but I continue to put my faith in God's miraculous power.

I believe that God can completely heal my ear! I don't say that because I'm a pastor or it looks good as I'm writing this book, but because I completely believe it to be true. I don't say this in a way that only focuses on my theological thoughts on the omnipotence of God, but I truly believe He knows me as His son and that He can heal me and desires it. I know what you're thinking, "Then why hasn't He healed you yet?" I'm not sure, but that doesn't change my belief in His ability to heal me, nor does it change my belief that He wants to heal me. I don't have all the answers, but I don't need to know, I just need to have faith.

Unless God tells you to stop praying for a miracle like He did to Paul, I encourage you to keep praying! Jesus tells us throughout the Gospels to pray (in faith) for healing, and that's all that I need to know. I'm going to leave the theology part up to God, and maybe one day in Heaven we'll know the whole story of why He chose not to answer a certain prayer, but until then, we need to keep putting our faith in God and believe He can move any mountain in our way.

I love this quote from Pastor Mark Batterson: "God isn't offended by your biggest dreams or boldest prayers. He is offended by anything less. If your prayers aren't impossible to you, they are insulting to God."

Maybe we're not seeing as many miracles because we're not praying as big of prayers. I want to live with God-sized faith and believe in God-sized miracles, and there's nothing that can stop me from praying and believing in these things. I'm still praying for my family and friends, still praying for my ear, still praying for revival in this land, and still have faith that Jesus is coming again!

Do you have FAITH when you're against the ropes?

ROUND 2: FAMILY

It is impossible to fight the spiritual fight alone. You need FAMILY because it's much easier to develop spiritual GRIT when you have them by your side!

FAMILIES FIGHT

You see, family is one of those words that immediately brings a smile or frown to your face depending on who you're talking to. For some, the word is refreshing, and it brings joy to you thinking about how blessed you've been throughout your life, and you can't help but praise God for the family you have. *For others, you don't even want to read this section because it brings a* bitter taste to your mouth because you're reminded of the life that you didn't have growing up.

Regardless of your personal experiences, you need to understand that family is one of God's greatest gifts to us. Again, for some of you, this is a no-brainer because you view this through the lens of your amazing experiences with your family. For the record, don't feel guilty if this is you. This is what it should be like! We need more Godly families paving the way so we can model for our children, as well as others, the examples they need. However, others of you haven't yet had healing from your family trauma and you still don't understand the importance of it. You might understand it as a concept, but you don't understand it as being something you need for yourself. If that's you, don't feel bad by reading this, but rather, open your heart to what God wants to do in this area.

Let me clarify, I've been there, trust me! In fact, I'm still there at times. God has done amazing work in my heart as well as worked in many of my family member's lives, but there are still times that this is a pain point for me. So, what does this have to do with fighting our spiritual fight and developing grit, right? Let's look at what the Word of God says.

Ephesians 6:12 NLT 12 "For we are not fighting against flesh-and-blood enemies, but against evil rulers and authorities of the unseen world, against mighty powers in this dark world, and against evil spirits in the heavenly places."

I quoted this earlier, but here I want to look at it in greater detail. Again, Paul is pointing out that we are in a spiritual fight, and he wants us to recognize who the enemy is and who it isn't. Some of you are convinced that the person who hurt you the worst is your enemy, but I want to suggest to you that he/she isn't. Before you get too upset and put this book down, hang on just a second. Coming from a broken home myself, I carried bitterness and hatred around for years, so I understand why one might think that those who've hurt us are the enemy, but they aren't. Satan is.

I'm not suggesting that they get a pass and can play the "devil made me do it" card, but I am saying that they can be influenced by him. If someone is not a born-again believer then he/she has a "veil" over their eyes (spiritually) and they can't see that they aren't living for God, which results in living sinful lives. I know what some of you are thinking, "They should have known to not say or do what they did to me," and you might be right, but others are so deceived by the enemy that they truly don't know. Meanwhile, some of you are thinking, "My parents were Christians, but they still did it." To that I say, I'm sorry that they didn't reflect God's love for you. Whether or not they acted in their flesh or were never truly saved I'm not sure, but what I do know is that it breaks God's heart when His children are not loved the way He desires for them to be.

However, we must get to the point where we realize that our battle is not with those who've hurt us, but with good and evil. Again, mankind's sinfulness can be at work, and it is not evil itself (but even that has evil roots), but Paul knew that Satan would trick us and hold us in bondage with hate towards our family members (and others). Paul was persecuted relentlessly, yet he still knew who his actual enemy was.

When Jesus was nailed to the cross, He asked the Father to forgive them, for they didn't know what they were doing. He was not referring to them not being aware of them nailing Him to the cross, but rather they didn't understand the spiritual implications at hand. Again, some might say, "Yeah, but that was Jesus." Okay, what about Stephen who was the first martyr? He says almost the same words as Jesus (Acts 7:60). They weren't giving them a pass to do whatever they wanted to them, but rather they knew they were in the center of God's will and that they were in a spiritual fight, so they wanted forgiveness to be extended to them so that their "eyes would be opened" and they too could have the same forgiveness from God that they experienced.

The Apostle Paul knew this all too well because he was at Stephen's stoning. The Book of Acts says, "And dragged him out of the city and began to stone him. His accusers took off their coats and laid them at the feet of a young man named Saul" (Acts 7:58). Before he was the Apostle Paul, he was Saul of Tarsus who opposed the name of Jesus, and he jailed and killed Christians. Jesus radically changed him on his way to persecute more Christians (Acts 9), and he ended up being the man who wrote the majority of the New Testament. Most believers are familiar with this, yet I'm not sure how many comprehend how difficult it would have been to accept Saul initially.

In fact, the disciples didn't believe him at first (Acts 9), but even when they believed it, they were faced with the decision to forgive him or not. After all, they watched their beloved friend be killed and Saul was behind it! They do forgive him, though, because the words of Jesus rang in their ears, "Father forgive them, for they do not know what they do." You can see why Paul knew it was important to address the spiritual warfare issue at hand when it comes to knowing who our enemy is and who it isn't, because what if the disciples refused to forgive him? Our Bibles would look a whole lot different than they do and there wouldn't have been nearly as many churches planted! The disciples not only forgave Paul, but they loved him and took him in as one of their own. They developed a brotherhood (2 Peter 3:15). As a result of this, Paul arguably became the greatest threat against the power of darkness, even more than the original disciples!

So, you see, if we don't learn to forgive, we can miss out on what God wants to do through those who've hurt us. More than that though, if we don't forgive, we allow the enemy to continue to win in our own lives because the hate and bitterness are eating us up.

It's been said, "Unforgiveness is like drinking our own poison and hoping the other person gets sick." We are not winning the fight with others when we hold on to bitterness, in fact, we are losing. Jesus' forgiveness for our sins is what defeated Satan's attack on us, and in return, we defeat Satan as well when we forgive those who have hurt us because it reminds him that he's already been defeated, and all he can do now is try to weaken the church with things like this. When the believers grow in their faith and learn to forgive their family, they begin to develop spiritual grit that allows them to keep fighting.

FAMILY BONDS

I grew up an only child for most of my life, but I had a cousin that was the same age as me that was as close as a brother. Every Friday after another long week of school, I would get picked up from school and immediately go to his house so that we could hang out together. We did this almost every single week from elementary school, all the way up until High School, and everyone knew this. We started as ornery little kids just messing around playing video games, watching tv, and cruising the streets on our bicycles thinking we ruled the world. Like any "brothers," we had our occasional fights and would get annoyed with each other (especially the time I ruined his brand-new pair of sneakers), but we knew we had each other's backs no matter what.

We had a true brotherhood, and we would do anything for each other. We both had rough home lives and were exposed to things that kids shouldn't ever see, so we learned to be there for each other through it all, even though we never really talked about what was going on. It was such a normal part of our lives we didn't think much of it because that's the way it had always been. We shared an unbreakable bond not just because we shared the same blood, but because we shared hard experiences, and we knew we weren't alone.

In my first book, *Never Going Back*, I tell the story about how my cousin tragically passed away from a drug overdose, and there's not a day that goes by that I don't think of him along with all the memories I had with him. Even though we weren't the best examples for each other, we did the best we knew how with the information that we had as well as the example set for us. My cousin was truly what Proverbs means when it says, "A brother is born to help in time of need" (Proverbs 17:17). Since his passing, I've been more motivated to show the love of God to others around me so that people who are struggling know there's someone here for them. Are you aware of those around you who need you to be a part of their "family"?

The older I've gotten, the more I've realized the importance of the family bond, and the more I discover God's heart for it. I have three younger siblings who are considered "half-siblings" (since we only share one parent), but they aren't any less of a sibling to me than if we shared the same set of parents. I know all situations are different, but my point is that my bond with them surpasses our family makeup. I love them all the same even though they are all different. I've had the opportunity to play a father figure to them all due to different circumstances, and it's been one of the greatest callings of my life. I've been able to build them up when they are down, challenge them when they need to be brought down a little, help them financially, and show them my support by attending their games or taking them out to eat.

Never once in being there for them have I thought this was a burden or wished someone else was there for them, instead, I was honored to have the chance to step into the gap for them because they needed me. Our upbringing had been much different than those around us and I'm the oldest of us all, and it's my responsibility to come alongside them and show them the way so that they can see an example of a Godly life. I'm certainly not perfect, and I don't try to be their parent, but I also know that I can provide something that is lacking in their lives.

This doesn't mean that it doesn't get challenging at times. When they don't talk or act like I want them to (and I know that the lack of parental guidance contributes to a lot of it) it can be very frustrating. However, this is where God reminds me that it's His role to shape them into who He's called them to be, it's only my role to model it for them. This doesn't mean that I don't speak my mind (though this has bit me in the butt at times), but my main job is to show them the love of the Heavenly Father.

Your situation is probably different from mine, but I bet you can relate to having people who look up to you and count on you. There's a family bond attached to people you love and would do anything for. This type of love flows from God, and it's a love that we're called to show to each other. Whether the people are biological or not, we need to help step up for others and stand in the gap.

Everyone is in a spiritual fight, whether they realize it or not, and God will use us to help someone by being in their corner when they need it the most. As I said, this can be difficult at times, and they might never thank us, but that's okay because we're not doing it for their approval. We're doing it because we love them with no strings attached. It's one thing to love them when they are making the decisions you want them to make, and it's another to continue to love them even when you don't agree with their decisions. Many people quit helping others because they feel like they've been "shorted" by them. After all, the person isn't doing what the person who helped them wants them to do. The love for those who have strayed away from the faith or even may have never put their faith in God, should always remain.

This doesn't mean we trust everyone the same, in fact, if we don't set up boundaries then we can hurt them and us. Once trust is broken it must be earned. However, God's love for that person must remain. We don't help them so that we can get something from them or take credit for helping them, we do it because we know God asked us to. Regardless of your story, when you've received the love of God, you now have the knowledge and experience of something that everyone else desires, and we can show it to them. God doesn't give up on us in our worst times, and we shouldn't give up on anyone else either. Develop family bonds that are centered on God's love and stand in the gaps for those who need it the most.

Maybe you're reading this, and you're reminded of a family member who's no longer here with you, and you reflect on the memories that you've had with them. Perhaps others of you think about a sibling (or other relative) that you have many cherished moments with, and you wonder why you're not as close to them as you once were. This can happen for a multitude of reasons, but one of the main reasons this happens is that we get busy in life, and we forget to check in and see how each other is doing. One of you moved away, got married, and had kids, and it's not until the next holiday that you realize you're just not as close to them as you once were. Don't let the enemy beat you up!

I have gone through seasons of checking out from other relationships where I knew I needed to be doing a better job of showing the love of Christ, but I felt so bad for not being there for them that I kept not doing anything about it. Finally, I realized that all I had to do was humble myself, reach out, and begin to strengthen the relationships again. More times than not the person is just glad you reached out again, and you pick up where you left off. Other times, you can apologize for not doing a better job of reaching out, and you ask for their forgiveness. This can be a powerful sign of your love for God and them because it's admitting that you're not perfect, and that God is still working on you.

SPIRITUAL FAMILY

What's amazing about the term "family" in Scripture is that it's not just bio-logical. We see this when Jesus is speaking to the crowds and someone tells him that his mother and brothers are there to see him, but he doesn't respond with how one might think he would!

Matthew 12:48-50 NLT

"48 Jesus asked, 'Who is my mother? Who are my brothers?' 49 Then he pointed to his disciples and said, 'Look, these are my mother and brothers. 50 Anyone who does the will of my Father in heaven is my brother and sister and mother!'"

Jesus wasn't being hateful towards his family, but he was teaching the importance of the Spiritual family. When we are saved into the family of God (adopted), we take on the name of Christ, hence the term "Christians." We are all sons and daughters of God the Father, and our relationship with God is more important than any other relationship. For those who have stories like mine, this makes sense and it's exciting because we are on the same level as everyone else.

This was demonstrated to me when my Godparents took me in and treated me as if I were their own. Even their kids loved and accepted me and shared their biological parents with me! Jesus did the same thing for us when He gave us access to the Father through the Holy Spirit by dying for our sins. Romans 8:15 NLT says, "So you have not received a spirit that makes you fearful slaves. Instead, you received God's Spirit when he adopted you as his own children. Now we call him, 'Abba, Father.'" It's incredible that Jesus gave us access to the Father by coming to Earth and dying for our sins! If we only ever see this as a theological idea, then we will never comprehend the love that the Father truly wants to show all of His children.

When the church (the people of God) begins to realize that we are sons and daughters (brothers and sisters), then it changes the way we view one another. When believers gather for church together on Sundays, there should be joy and excitement that comes with seeing one another. Unfortunately, this is typically not the case for most Christians. Church has become optional, and I believe it's because we don't have a good understanding of what church is. I'm a pastor, so I feel like I have some equity in saying this, but the church was not formed by coming, singing a few songs, listening to a sermon, and then leaving before anyone corners you. The church was built on genuine relationships that formed a faith community that focused on breaking down the words of Jesus, companionship, and eating together (amen!) (Acts 2:42).

For the record, this is not my attempt at criticizing the church, but I do feel many Christians have missed this significant aspect of what it means to be part of the Christian community.

People often ask me how I was able to turn from my old lifestyle and Never Go Back (shameless book plug). I always answer with the same response, "Jesus, fried fish and taters, and Diet Dr. Pepper (very healthy, I know)." Normally, the person who asked me that question looks at me with a confused look on their face, and rightfully so. I always use this as an opportunity to share with them the importance of having a strong spiritual family around them.

I go on to tell them the rest of the story about how my youth pastors allowed me to hang around with them until late in the night and they asked me questions (as we ate fish and taters and drank Diet Dr. Pepper) and they showed me the love of Jesus. They genuinely cared and asked me questions that no one else asked me before. Many people understood that I came from a dysfunctional family and that my choices weren't good, but no one asked me the deeper questions until then. They were so glad that I put my faith in Jesus, but they also wanted to help me by coming alongside me and helping meet my needs. I had never experienced anything like this before, and to be honest, it was uncomfortable at first. They didn't make me uncomfortable with what they said or did, but their love was different from any other love that I had ever experienced. It was truly "out of this world."

I share the whole story about how they became my Godparents and helped me become who I am today in my other book, but what I will say is they took a chance on me when no one else did, and that's exactly what Jesus desires the Church to do. It was the love and forgiveness of Jesus that saved me, but it was the love and acceptance of the Church that sustained me.

Some of you read this and think to yourself, "That's great that you had that wonderful experience, but that's not my story with the Church," and to that, I say I'm sorry. Truly, I'm sorry that no one ever stepped up to help you the way that you needed, but don't let that keep you from being a part of the community that you need today. Regardless of how old you are, we all need community because we are not meant to do life alone. Since the beginning of time, "it's not good for man to be alone," and this still applies today. God demonstrated the importance of community after Pentecost and the development of the Early Church by showing us His desire to see the Church live life together.

"46 They worshiped together at the Temple each day, met in homes for the Lord's Supper, and shared their meals with great joy and generosity— 47 all the while praising God and enjoying the goodwill of all the people. And each day the Lord added to their fellowship those who were being saved" (Acts 2:46-47 NLT).

Did you notice the focus on community here? The Church was just born, and Luke makes sure to add the fact that the people of God were enjoying each other's company. There were components of reading the Scriptures and partaking in the Lord's Supper, but there were also people of God hanging out and enjoying each other's company.

I think sometimes Christians forget that it's not a sin to have fun! The "world" likes to act like Christians are boring and don't know how to have a good time (and in some ways they are right), but I believe Christians should have the most fun together. I lived the life the world promised would be fun, and it was for a season, until it left me empty and unfulfilled. With God, we get to live life to the fullest and enjoy God's amazing creation by having fun and doing things that bring joy to our lives, but through the lens that they are blessings from God (James 1:17). God knows how to have fun because He created it, and He desires for His children to experience His blessings and have fun with one another.

After I got saved, my youth pastors not only took me in as my new family and provided for me, but they were also some of the most fun people I'd ever been around! I began to get introduced to other Godly people who liked to have fun as well, and it blew my mind that I never knew life could be this way! No worry of getting in trouble, no worry if we would die from our actions (except the excessive sodium from fish as well as aspartame from the diet soda), no regrets the next day, just good, Godly fun!

Before my cousin passed away from his drug relapse, I introduced him to my new God-Family and friends, and he couldn't believe that we had the joy that we had as well as the amount of fun we were having. We grew up having a lot of fun together, but because we didn't know Jesus, there was always an emptiness inside of us, but then there we were all those years later, having more fun than ever before.

I remember one night we had gone to watch one of our friends in the youth group play in a high school basketball game, and it was a night filled with laughter to the point that it hurt! We had great food, great music, great conversations, and just all-around great fun. When we were all in the car driving home, I looked back to see how my cousin was doing in the back of the car (with all these new people he had just met), and he was covering his face with his hands and tears were flowing down his arms. About this time, everyone calmed down and noticed what was going on and we all got quiet.

"You alright, cuz?" I asked. He nodded but he couldn't speak because he was so choked up. My cousin wasn't a crier, and he was one tough dude, so it was very abnormal to see him like this.

After a few seconds of silence, he finally gathered himself and said, "I didn't know this existed, cuz. I didn't know you could have this."

I knew exactly what he meant because it was the same overwhelming feeling that I felt once I got around my new church friends, and now my cousin was experiencing the same exact thing. I invited him many times before he eventually agreed to come because I wanted him to experience the love of a Godly community. The bond that we had all the years before was real, but it wasn't what we were experiencing at that moment because the love back then wasn't rooted in God. We can experience good relationships with people, but they will always be incomplete if they are not rooted in God's love. It doesn't mean we still can't have fun with others who don't follow God, but there's a clear distinction in Scripture between community with believers and non-believers, and we need to be wise with our relationships. With that being said, we need to show love to those who don't know God so that they can experience His love, just like my cousin did. If we never show them God's love, how will they ever know what it feels/looks like?

The sad part of this story is that after watching my cousin get saved and having the chance to baptize him, he fell back into his addiction and tragically passed away. It still breaks my heart to this day, but I know that I did everything I could to make sure he knew we loved him and were still there for him. His death motivated me to be more passionate than before to make sure that I love on those around me, so they know there's always someone here for them. Just like my cousin and me, they crave community, and they are either going to get it from the world or from the Church, and it's the Church's responsibility to welcome people with open arms, ask the questions no one else is asking, and make them feel like they have spiritual family that's there for them.

NOT JUST FRIENDS, BUT FAMILY

When we were in middle school, my cousin (along with other friends) would go to the mall on the weekends and spend most of the day there, walking around with polos with popped collars and fake white Gucci sunglasses, and we thought we were the coolest kids ever (it was cool at the time, trust me... so we thought). None of us had any money to spend so we had no intentions of buying anything, and when it got to be lunchtime, we would get as many food samples as we could from the Chinese restaurant until they finally cut us off.

As the day went on, we would walk by the other middle school boys who were roaming around, and we would have the famous "stare down" with them which signified that we were ready to fight if they wanted to. I'm now fully aware of how ridiculous it sounds that a bunch of middle school boys walked around with popped collars and fake luxury white sunglasses looking for a fight, but at the time, we were the toughest kids in town, just ask us! As we got older, the same thing would happen (though our dress would evolve into the newest embarrassing trend) everywhere we went, and it seemed like we were constantly getting into trouble.

Still to this day, I can't go to the mall, the fair, and other places that my friends and I went to without thinking about how immature we were, but I also think about the power of friendship. We were all considered troubled kids that came from troubled homes, and these moments were when we would escape from our situations, and we felt powerful together. We were all filled with pain and anger and lacked parental direction, so when we would roam the streets together, it was our opportunity to conquer the world and be a part of an unbreakable bond, and we knew we had each other's back no matter what. If you messed with one of us, then you messed with all of us. We weren't just friends, we were family.

Though we didn't know it at the time, what we wanted was to be a part of something bigger than ourselves, and nothing is ever as good when you're just by yourself. When big things happen in your life, you want to share it with others so they can celebrate with you. The opposite is true as well. When you find yourself in a hard situation, you eventually realize that it would be helpful to you to talk to someone else about what you're going through. The problem is when we don't understand who created us, then we won't know why we are here, and we spend our lives looking to be a part of things that make us feel noticed and needed. This is why people find themselves a part of groups that participate in outrageous things, because their desire to be a part of something bigger than themselves can make their vision cloudy and do things they never thought they would end up doing.

Going back to my middle school days, this is when a thing called "peer pressure" was introduced in a powerful way. This is the time in people's lives when they decide who they want to be and what they want to do. Up to this point, most kids are relatively the same when it comes to behaviors and decisions (though not always true), but when puberty is underway and new temptations arise, it forces people to decide what path to go on, and this is where friendship is essential. For my friends and I, we were negative influences on each other, and it led us to continue to make worse decisions the older we got. For others, their decision to befriend people is the thing that helps them grow closer to God and they are positive influences in their lives. I can almost guarantee you that if you look back on your life and evaluate the decisions you've made, there's a direct correlation between them and your friends. For me, I had to make changes within my friend group to become the man of God that I am now, but it wasn't easy. I loved my friends, but once I realized my identity as a child of God, I knew I needed to be around those who shared the same values.

For me, my identity was tied up in my image of being "cool, tough, and athletic," and if you didn't fit into one of those categories, then I couldn't be associated with you because you would hurt my image. The irony of this is that my image was terrible, but I had convinced myself (more like been deceived) that I was better than I really was. So, once I became a new Christian, I had to let go of my old image to receive my new image, which was a Jesus follower. Many people don't understand this principle, though. When we become a new creation (2 Corinthians 5:17), our identity is not in who we used to be, but who we are now. This doesn't only apply to our old sins, but it's also the "good things" we were a part of such as "athlete, popular, tough, etc." It doesn't mean these things are bad and it doesn't mean those things aren't still true, but they lose their meaning in our lives. In other words, they aren't what's most important to me. Jesus is what's most important to me, not your perception of how cool (or not so cool) you think I am.

Do you understand how freeing this is? You would think that this is only a teenage thing, but that's not true at all! It doesn't matter how old you are, we will continue to look for people and other things to validate us. Don't believe me? Why do grown men follow the strongest person in the gym around like he's Arnold Schwarzenegger? Why do grown women want to be around the prettiest girl in town with the most followers on social media? Because the little boy and little girl inside us want to be connected with people that we think will make us feel more meaningful, but in all reality, it doesn't make us more meaningful, it makes us miserable. When we choose to get our meaning in anyone other than God, then we will always be let down because we will always try to keep up with the status quo.

Regardless of the path you might have chosen, we can agree that there's power in friendship. The good news is, that it's never too late to make the changes you need to make and develop new friendships that will help you grow closer to God. When we understand that God is the one who created us, and the reason why we are here is to have a relationship with Him and to be a part of the family of God, it frees us from the empty pursuit of trying to find meaning with anyone that will accept us.

FAMILY SUPPORT

God created friendships, and we see examples of Godly friendships through-out the Bible. Friends are God's gift to mankind to help us get through the trials of life. When you decide to follow God and go in a different direction than your friends, it's a scary place to be in initially because you don't have familiar faces around you. Your influence and connection are no longer established with those people, and you have to choose to put your trust in God and believe He will provide what you need, or you will ultimately go back to what's familiar and go back to doing what you've always done with your old friends.

This is one of the most challenging things for people because their identity is so tied up in their friends that they can't imagine no longer having them in their lives. Again, Jesus never said it was easy to follow Him. This is where many people give up on their spiritual fight and choose to go back to their old ways. However, the ones who choose to stay committed to following Jesus, develop spiritual grit that enables them to be stronger than they ever were before and realize that they don't need the things of this world to give them meaning. As you continue to be faithful to the call of God, many of those who you used to hang out with will eventually reach out to you, wanting what you now have, or at least respect you for who you have become.

When we choose to obey God, He will always provide the friends that we need, but we must welcome them. I can attest to this in every season I've been in! When we give up people or things for God's sake, He will always provide who or what we need to stay strong in the spiritual fight. In my experience, God often sends you people that you wouldn't have ever guessed would become great friends to you. This doesn't mean that Jesus is the only thing you have in common with them, though. If you like sports, then God will send you people who like sports also, if you like music then He'll send you people who like music as well; however, sometimes the only thing you have in common with them is your faith, and that's awesome!

That's what's amazing about the family of God. We're not limited to liking only those who are exactly like us, but our faith connects us with people we wouldn't have ever picked out of a crowd. What we discover is that God puts people in our path who think and act differently than us to reveal His creativity, and we begin to appreciate the differences in others rather than be repulsed by them. In fact, we become stronger in our walk with God because we have others who sharpen us in ways that we haven't been sharpened yet.

Maybe you haven't had positive experiences with friends within the Church and it's caused you to lose faith in the Church and you feel lonelier now than ever before. If that's you, I urge you to not give up, and continue to try to connect with other Christians in your faith community and pray that God will send you more Godly friends.

We are meant to do life together and we need each other more than ever. As the world becomes increasingly darker, you must find a strong group of believers to come alongside you, hold each other accountable, and pour into each other. If not, we leave ourselves susceptible to the enemy's attacks and end up with no one around us watching our backs when we are the most vulnerable.

If you think that you're strong enough on your own, I can assure you that you're not. If you don't find this community to surround yourself with, then the enemy can speak to you more clearly because there are no other voices around helping you listen to God. You might be able to be strong for a bit, but not for long. That's why the Bible says, "A person standing alone can be attacked and defeated, but two can stand back-to-back and conquer. Three are even better, for a triple-braided cord is not easily broken" (Ecclesiastes 4:12 NLT).

One of the main reasons a boxer has a team with him/her is to help them stay concentrated on the end goal, which is to win the fight! This consists of keeping them accountable for their diet, decisions, training, friend groups, and much more. If the fighter loses focus, then they might begin to cut corners in one of these areas, but the team holds them accountable and reminds them of why they are doing what they are doing. It's not fun to be held accountable at first, but eventually, you grow to love it and even crave it because you want to be the best you can be. Some Christians are fine with going through the motions and they think that they are "just fine" the way they are, and they are exactly right. They are "just fine," not bad, not good, just fine. I don't believe for a second that's what God desires for His people. I believe that He wants sold-out people who are committed to paying the cost to follow Him and who want to be the best "fighters" against evil that they can be. To do this though, you need people in your corner!

FAMILY (FRIENDS) IN LOWLY PLACES

Have you ever realized how much better bad situations are when you have friends around? No one necessarily enjoys bad situations, but when there are others by your side, you're reminded that you're not alone.

Going back to the Apostle Paul, he found himself in a lot of bad situations. Not because of his own bad decisions, but because he followed Jesus wholeheartedly. In Acts 16, he finds himself in another prison cell after casting out a demon, which, once again, affirms my point about our fight against good and evil. This time though, Silas (another Jesus follower) is with him. Before being put in the cell, they were stripped and severely beaten, and now they were there with their feet locked and clamped down so they couldn't move.

I think it's safe to admit that this is not the image that comes to mind when we think about following Jesus, but this was their reality. I also think it's safe to admit that if you or I were in that situation we would be terrified. Perhaps they were scared as well, but that's not what I see when I read the story.

"25 Around midnight Paul and Silas were praying and singing hymns to God, and the other prisoners were listening. 26 Suddenly, there was a massive earthquake, and the prison was shaken to its foundations. All the doors immediately flew open, and the chains of every prisoner fell off! 27 The jailer woke up to see the prison doors wide open. He assumed the prisoners had escaped, so he drew his sword to kill himself. 28 But Paul shouted to him, 'Stop! Don't kill yourself! We are all here!'" (Acts 16:25-28).

Instead of begging and pleading with the guards to let them out and promising to not speak about the name of Jesus any longer, they got louder! Where does this type of faith come from? Well, the obvious answer is God, and that's correct. However, I think there's more to the story here. I think that the other thing at play is the spiritual grit that came from various trials they had experienced beforehand (at least for Paul), along with the fact that they had each other. Their spiritual family bond was unbreakable in a situation that was designed to break them.

Where the jailers went wrong was leaving them together! If they wanted to try to get them to stop talking about Jesus, they should have separated them, though I think Paul had too much grit to quit. When they were in a difficult situation, they chose to praise God instead of cursing Him. It's one thing for Paul to heal people when people think he's a god (Acts 14:12), it's another when people want to kill you. Paul didn't do what he did for the approval of people, though. He knew he was there to share the Gospel. Instead, they begin praying and singing hymns together, and the Scriptures say that the other prisoners were listening. I love this! It's tempting to think that unbelievers don't care about how we live our lives, but they do, at least when we are being the salt and light.

The other prisoners were there for actual crimes unlike Paul and Silas, and here they are living out their faith at the bottom of the prison. I believe the other prisoners were intrigued by them because they possibly had heard of them before, and even if not, they were intrigued by their joy in a bad situation. Same situation, different types of people, different responses. This is why Paul says, "Always be joyful. Never stop praying. Be thankful in all circumstances, for this is God's will for you who belong to Christ Jesus" (1 Thessalonians 5:16-17). When we are thankful in hard moments, it shows that our faith is not based on our feelings, but on our belief in God and His plans. Like Paul and Silas, we too must have faith in our prison season because it can lead to other people putting their faith in God as well, and that's exactly what happens (read the whole story).

The praise of Paul and Silas caused the chains on them to fall off and they were free to go. Let me remind you, praise is a weapon against the enemy, and when we give Him praise in our low moments, our chains will fall off and we, too, will be free! I can't help but visualize them at that moment and wonder who began to sing first. It just says they both were singing and praying, so we're not sure who started it. I'm guessing they didn't just begin singing and praying out loud at the same time after one of them counted them in like an orchestra conductor, but instead, one began to sing and then the other joined along. It doesn't necessarily matter who started first, and I'm not suggesting who did it was Godlier, but I do think it's important to point out that praise is not only a weapon, but it's also contagious.

When one person begins to praise God, others will praise Him. The opposite is true as well. When one begins to complain to or about God, others will do the same, and we can end up finding ourselves stuck in our chains, all because of who we are around. In Paul and Silas' case, their freedom came because they were praising God together. I know it was God who freed them, but did you notice they were still in chains until they began to praise? Paul had Silas, and Silas had Paul. Paul is the most known out of the two, but it took both in this instance to be set free to continue in their spiritual fight.

Paul most likely wasn't going to quit, but let's act as if he was going to. Let's pretend that he had enough of the beatings and persecution for his faith. Perhaps the company of Silas comforted him enough to keep being strong. What if Silas began to pray or praise first and he was reminded to keep going? No matter how strong you are, we all get tired, and we can benefit from having others around. Or maybe his seeing Silas was a reminder that he knew it was important to be strong in his faith so that he could continue to strengthen his fellow family of believers. Regardless of who started praying and praising first, their family bond that was rooted in their faith in Jesus led to them being set free, and they kept persevering together.

I want you to think about who you have as your Paul and Silas in your own life. When you find yourself at the bottom of a prison (literally or figuratively), who do you call? Who's in your corner? Another question is, are they who you should be calling? Are they rooted in Christ? Truly? Sometimes we must give up friendships to gain our Paul or Silas. If you're still bitter over the fact that you don't have someone, then you need to possibly look in the mirror and ask yourself if you've been a good family member to other believers, or perhaps even your own biological family. God can restore any situation, but it might take some time. Invite people into your corner who will help sharpen you and hold you accountable. Get someone who will challenge you to begin to praise God even though you feel like giving up.

We need family to keep on going in the spiritual fight, and it's going to take a whole lot of grit to keep going, but you're not alone.

CHEERING ON THE FAMILY

Did you ever have a time when an older sibling, relative, or friend taught you something new and was happy for you, and it was fun to begin to bond over it? It starts off as a fun bonding experience and then suddenly, you get to where you can beat them and then it's not as "bonding" as it was at first. When you first begin playing you both are laughing over your ignorance of the new hobby and then when you begin to learn it you rejoice together, and then it begins to be a competition and no longer words are being spoken (or if they are they are for mouthing purposes only).

After moving in with my Godparents, I learned to play ping-pong with Jon (my God-dad), and I thought it was the lamest thing I had ever played. He encouraged me to stay with it and eventually, I began to like it even though I wasn't any good yet. Then, one day it clicked for me, and I began to go head-to-head with him. At first, he was happy for me and congratulated me, and then I FINALLY won a game! Then another. And another. Suddenly, Jon wasn't so happy for me, and we found ourselves going at it for hours as we battled it out.

After beating him again, he yelled out in frustration, "I've beat you 1,000 times!!!"

I tried my best not to laugh but I couldn't help it. Not because it was funny (though it was… he's hilarious), but because I finally figured it out and was able to hold my own. I grew more and more confident in my ping-pong skills (some would even say cocky, and I would agree), and then suddenly, I found myself teaching the younger teens in the youth group to play. I learned during that time how patient Jon was with me because teaching teens how to play is extremely taxing!

Then one day, IT happened. I was playing with one of the younger guys (who I used to beat with my opposite hand), and I realized that he was pretty good. He was really good. Oh wow, he's better than me. After losing, I brushed it off like it was no big deal and like I didn't care (but really, I was ready to challenge this kid half my size to fight). At that moment, I realized the irony of my time playing ping-pong with Jon and now being beaten by someone I had helped learn the game. It's one thing to cheer for someone when you're better than them, but how about when they are better than you?

I learned this principle early on in ministry when some older pastors reached out to encourage me and tell me they believed in me. As time went on, God was growing me into a leader and began to open doors, and I found myself doing things that I never dreamed of doing. I found myself sitting at tables I never imagined I could sit at, and I realized that the people who first encouraged me weren't doing it any longer. In fact, it was the opposite. At first, I brushed it off thinking it was just a bad interaction, but the longer time went on, the more I realized there was something more.

As I opened up to an older and wiser pastor, they told me something I'll never forget. "Dylan, nothing is more intimidating to an older person than youth. I know it's hard for you to understand, but one day you will."

When I heard this, I took a step back and realized the similarity of the ping-pong situation. It's one thing for us to start off learning something, but once we begin to develop in that area, it's much harder (for some, not all) to want to continue to encourage us. I don't say that in a naïve or arrogant way that suggests I'm so good that some can't stand to even see my face. There were things I probably could have done or said better to make sure to not present myself in a certain way that would cause someone to dislike me. At the same time, it was a good lesson for me to learn, because one day I was going to be the leader who looked at the younger up-and-coming leaders, and I needed to decide then how I would treat them.

Funnily enough, it didn't take me getting much older to feel this! It didn't take long to realize that when you've done something "successful" like leading a large youth group, planting a church, or speaking at a lot of events, people quit telling you "Good job." However, when the new guy/girl on the block shows up and does something "successful," it's the best new thing out there, and you're old news. I realized that I had a decision to make. Will I embrace the success of the other person, or will I reject it? If we embrace them then we can be in their corner and help them in their spiritual fight. If we reject them, then we will not be in their corner, and we can miss out on helping them grow into the leaders they are called to be. In some cases, you can miss out on something even bigger than what you thought you were supposed to be a part of yourself because God was going to do more through them than you. That can discourage you, or it can encourage you by knowing you've done your part. I love what my God-mom and pastor often quotes, "Let my fruit grow on other people's trees."

The irony of me feeling this way towards others at times is that I am the poster child for someone who has been given all the help in the world, and if it wasn't for others, I would have never been able to experience the things I have or will experience in the future. So, why in the world would I be so entitled to think that I'm the only one that God wants to use? Instead of growing distant from those people (whether I know them from afar or up close), I want to welcome them and give them everything I can! People are in a spiritual fight and are constantly getting dragged down by the weight of the world and the critiques and comparisons of others, and the last thing they need is for someone who once built them up to disappear or even put them down. Did we actually love them and believe in them like we said if it's only based on us being better than them? That's a worldly "strings-attached" kind of love. God's love is unconditional, and it loves to celebrate others' success. God blessing others doesn't mean He won't bless you, because God doesn't run out of blessings like they are pieces of candy. However, if He sees you can't celebrate others' success, then He knows He can't trust you with more success because it's too much of an idol in your life. Cheer on the family of God and others will cheer you on!

I'm not sure there's a better example of this than the disciples' acceptance and support of Paul. They followed Jesus around for three years, started the Church (by the Holy Spirit's power), and were now prominent people after being nobodies in society, but God chose Paul to do more than all of them and he ended up writing two-thirds of the Bible. If you want to talk about an opportunity to become jealous and bitter, look no further than this one! For them, it's the opposite. They adopt Paul as a brother-in-Christ and cheer him on because they could so clearly see the calling on his life.

This is what it looks like to cheer on the family of God. They all did their part and God's church thrived because of it! This should challenge us today to repent of our competitiveness that leads to jealousy, anger, and bitterness. I'm as competitive as they come, and if you're like me, when you read that statement, you automatically size me up by thinking you're even more competitive than me! (I love it!) This can be a good thing in our spiritual fight, but if we're not careful, we can let our flesh, or the devil run with this and hinder the work of God through our lives. Notice how I didn't say "hinder the work of God" by itself. God's work will never be hindered by us, no matter how badly we mess up because He's that powerful; however, it can hinder us by robbing us of being a part of a move of God. If not you, then God will use someone else!

I do believe there are certain things that God wants to do only through you since there's only one person like you, but I do believe God will use someone else to accomplish His plans if you are not willing to embrace His plan. We must be held accountable by other brothers and sisters who are willing to call us out when we are blinded by the success of others to the point that we are developing a jealous spirit. This is exactly what we see in the life of King Saul and David, and we end up saying and doing things we never thought we would because of this spirit. To go deeper, if we give the enemy a foothold in this area then he can hold us captive and torment us. So, we need to confess to God, sometimes to the other person (though not always), and pray about this and ask God to give us a love for them and ask Him if there's something we can do to help them. Don't do this in a superficial way that isn't meaningful to you. God knows your motives. If you don't feel victory yet, then keep confessing and ask God to give you freedom, and you will.

One of the best ways to get freedom in this area is to not think about the other person's success but think about their greatest failure. Paradoxical, I know, but it works. When you think of them making the worst decision, he/she could because they didn't have a close person, (that could have possibly been you) it makes you sick, or it should. If that doesn't work, then think of Satan himself trapping them against the ropes and unloading a series of punches on them. If you've ever seen someone beat up badly, then you know it's not a "cool scene." Imagine hearing them gasp for a breath and barely having the air to cry out for help, and you hear them beginning to whimper as they are beaten unconscious. Graphic, I know. That's the point.

When you think of this, you should (as a Christian) desire to run over and help them. This is a metaphor, but it's closer to reality than you might realize. Oftentimes, some of the most gifted people we know are the most insecure because no one is there building them up when he/she isn't doing what they are known for. Sure, everyone is there when they are "performing" what they do best, but when they aren't then they often are in the spotlight getting critiqued. Look no further than celebrities and athletes. They are great at what they do, and people build them up, but in one second, everyone can tear them down. We need to be always there for people so that we can have deep and rich relationships that demonstrate the love that comes from being part of the family of God.

Before I end this section, I want to say one more thing on this topic. I remember Pastor Craig Groeschel once said, "When people stop congratulating you on something they used to consistently, just know you've gotten so consistent that they expect it." Wow. When I heard those words, it was with a sigh of relief. At first, we're looking for constant validation from anyone to tell us what we did was the best thing they've ever heard (and some did tell you that you were literally the best), and then we wait for the next validation. I believe we grow out of that stage eventually, to where we do what we do because God called us, equipped us, and assigned us to do it, and if no one else tells us "Good job," we know our Heavenly Father is proud of us.

YOUR FAMILY'S FUTURE

I can honestly say that I have the wife of my dreams! I know we say that sometimes as a formality to our spouse or others, but I truly mean it.

Growing up, I had no sense of what a Godly marriage or family looked like, and it wasn't until I lived with my God family that I knew what I wanted my marriage to look like. Not in the things that made them uniquely them, but in the way that God was the center of their marriage and they loved and valued each other so beautifully in a way that shows God's love. I knew that I was not going to settle on who I would spend the rest of my life with, and I didn't.

For me, I desired to have someone like a Proverbs 31 woman, but I wasn't sure if I would ever have it based on my past. As I continued to grow in The Lord, He began to change my thinking of myself and revealed to me that He also desired for me to have this type of wife, but I had to continue to grow in Him and focus on becoming the man of God He desired for me to be. It became increasingly clear that I knew the caliber of woman I wanted to spend the rest of my life with, and I wasn't going to settle either. As time went on, I met my future wife, Madi, and we eventually got married, and I couldn't believe that God gave me someone like her! Her story was the opposite of mine, but she didn't care, she just loved me for who I was in Christ, and I was someone that she desired as well. It blew my mind that someone like me could be desired by someone like her, but that's what God can do when someone is dedicated to God. She wasn't focused on who I used to be; she was focused on who I was now. All those years of following God prepared me to marry someone like her, and she was exactly the type of person I desired.

Psalm 37:4 "Take delight in the LORD, and he will give you your heart's desires."

This is our marriage verse because we truly believe that God gave us our heart's desires in each other!

We had five amazing years with just the two of us before having children. During this time, we not only got married, but were still in school, planted a church, traveled, and did evangelism together, and she accepted her call into ministry. We grew so close to one another during these years, and it allowed us to develop a closer relationship than ever. Looking back, there were a lot of hard moments that we had together as we were learning what it looked like to be married as well as all these other big life decisions that were happening. If God wasn't the center, I don't know how we would have gotten through some of the things that we did, both emotionally and physically. It wasn't because we were both in the ministry that we were able to grow closer to each other as well as grow in our faith in God, ministry was the byproduct of that. It was because we were both grounded individually in God which allowed our marriage to be grounded in God, which then allowed us to go to Him in everything we went through. Not that our marriage was bad, but we went through a lot of different things that put a lot of stress on our marriage, but we learned how to stop fighting each other, and fight together!

Madi is the best example I know of being kind. She smiles and greets people like they are the most important people to her, and she means it. She is present when she talks to people and isn't distracted by her phone or by the other people around (unless it's our kids climbing up her leg). She's a great listener and will give wise and Godly counsel back, or just hug you if that's what you need. Madi is a safe zone for me, our kids, and others. This trait of kindness is something that I value so deeply because I didn't see that a whole lot growing up. I never realized how much I appreciated this trait of hers until we had kids, and watching her be the mother to our children made me love and appreciate her even more as I get to watch our kids be shown the kindness that flows from the Holy Spirit (Galatians 5).

I believe that the Holy Spirit was putting desires in my heart, before I even met Madi, to show me the type of person I could spend the rest of my life with because He knew how important it is to have the right kind of person in your corner. Madi's love and kindness are something that I know I can rely on day in and day out, and she's my greatest teammate in life. Being a pastor, there are a lot of things that I know about and go through that I can't tell many people, but she's always there to help me go through whatever I need and is my constant support. Though she's sweet and caring, she's also extremely tough and strong-willed, and the perfect person to fight alongside me. We have our low moments just like anyone else, but we know that God brought us together and we know we are called to fight the spiritual fight alongside one another. Now that we have kids, our schedules look different, but we are still committed to putting God first, each other second, kids (and family) third, and then the ministry. We help each other develop grit by pushing each other forward in our faith, and we go to war against the enemy every day, and we still desire each other as much as ever.

There's no other relationship that is closer than your spouse, and that's because God designed it that way. There's no other person that we will be "one flesh" with (Mark 10:8-90). God created marriage and he desires it to be held in high regard, and one of those reasons is because He knows how much we need the other person. Unfortunately, many Christians don't utilize their marriages like God designed and they don't help each other (Genesis 2), but rather hurt each other.

I believe the enemy comes after our marriages so strongly because he knows the impact they can have when the couple is dedicated to God and His plans. When you spend so much time with someone like in a marriage, you can be in sync unlike any other relationship, or it can be the easiest way to let the enemy get in the middle and wreak havoc. When we lose sight of what God says about marriage and why we decided to get married, then we will naturally grow apart and learn to tolerate each other rather than thrive together. God desires Christians to have strong and healthy marriages that are committed to the spiritual fight together. This doesn't mean there's no romance and fun, in fact, these things are enhanced when a couple is committed to the spiritual fight! Satan will do everything he can to prevent your marriage from being strong because we aren't as strong when we're not united. One of the reasons I think this happens is because the dating season wasn't grounded in God.

Many Christians don't understand (or don't take seriously) the importance of Godly dating and go about it nonchalantly, and then years later when they have jobs, kids, and a mortgage, they begin to see sides of their spouse that they didn't know was there. So many couples struggle because God wasn't the center of their dating relationship and they assumed that it would all work out in the end, but this isn't always the case and it's not wise. I do believe that God can work all things out (Romans 8:28), but too often, people treat God like an escape button, and they choose to do whatever they want now and pray He will work it out later, but they aren't aware of the problems that can occur. This isn't to say that those who've kept God at the center since the beginning don't have problems, but it is much easier to grow in your relationship together from the beginning rather than trying to make it happen down the road.

When couples begin having families, a new and exciting feeling comes over them because there's a new person coming into the family mix! This is such a fun and exciting time for so many reasons, but it doesn't come without its challenges, just ask the mother who carried the child for nine months!

The moment a child is born, there is immediate joy, and the new parents are so proud of their new addition to the family. The first few weeks are thrilling and absolutely exhausting, but very bonding as well! As time goes on, and after a lot of sleep deprivation, couples begin to wonder, "Will life ever be the same again?" Nope, but it's amazing! If you're a new parent and are in this season, hang in there, you're going to be okay!

The thrill of becoming parents is such a joy, and they are so thankful for the new blessing they have, and many believe this is exactly what they need. However, for others, this is an overwhelming wake-up call to realize their marriage is going to take even more work now, and it wasn't working before this new child came who demands their attention twenty-four/seven at first. Unfortunately, for many, the marriage continues to get worse, not better. I've often seen the kids become the focal point of the marriage and the kids are the only thing that the couples have in common now. After years of growing apart, people don't even know the person that they created a child with. As the child gets older, they see Mom and Dad have a weak marriage and they assume that all marriages are like that, and then the cycle of unhealthy marriages continues with them. For some, addiction or adultery gets involved and this gets passed down to the kids, as well and a generational curse begins, and people come to expect the same thing from the next generation.

I know you're thinking, 'Well, that was depressing.' I know, but I've seen it more times than I can count. I also know that many of you are thinking that this is an extreme example, but I would argue that it's more prevalent now than ever. While not all Christian marriages fall into this, I do believe that many fall into the trap of simply living together and going through the motions. When couples are going through the motions together, they lose the fight for their marriage and then they just fight one another. Again, we all have a fighter spirit, but if we don't use it against the enemy, then we will use our fight for the wrong things. This is why so many couples spend so much time doing other things rather than focusing on their marriage because they want to use that fight towards things that fuel them. This is why jobs, hobbies, and other things become issues in marriages because the two aren't united together in their marriage and aren't committed to fighting together.

On the other hand, when the couple is united together and grounded in God, then they learn to fight together rather than fight each other. Have you ever seen a married couple like this? When you see two people grounded in God who work together as if they are on the same team rather than opposing teams, then they can accomplish so much more spiritually than marriages that aren't on the same page.

This changes the way that we view dating because we don't want to base our relationship on temporary things that potentially have the chance to limit our impact on the Kingdom once the honeymoon season fades. Many people who fit into this category are way past the dating phase and feel like it's too late for their marriage since they can't go back in time. Let me be clear, God can restore any relationship that is struggling, and it's never too late for God to redeem what the enemy has stolen and can use your marriage to be an example to others struggling.

Not only does God want to use marriages in the spiritual fight, but He also wants to use the children. I know we don't like to think about the idea of children being a part of spiritual warfare, but whether we like it or not, the enemy is no respecter of age. He comes for children just like parents. If you don't believe me, look at the current state of our children with depression and identity crisis. See, it's so crucial for parents to live out their faith in front of their children because if not, they won't be able to stay strong against the enemy's attacks. If Mom and Dad don't lead the kids spiritually, then the world would love to.

There's no such thing as a mediocre relationship with God because Jesus will spit us out of His mouth when we are "lukewarm" (Revelation 3). Many parents are willing to do whatever it takes to make life as good as possible for their kids, but that's only temporary. While it's a good thing to take care of our children by meeting their needs and showing them what it is they need to learn to be successful in life, there's nothing more important than leading our children in a way that sets them up for spiritual success.

As Christian parents, our children need to see a healthy marriage as well as the entire family living out our faith and being the Church rather than just going to church. If not, our children will grow up wanting the opposite of what they've seen. I believe the lack of spiritual leadership at home is one of the main causes for the "nones" (not catholic nuns) in this generation. In his book *The Nones*, author Ryan Burge writes:

"In 1972, just 5 percent of Americans claimed 'no religion' on the General Social Survey. In 2018, that number rose to 23.7 percent, making the nones as numerous as both evangelical Protestants and Roman Catholics. Every indication is that the nones will be the largest religious group in the United States in the next decade."[11]

He explains a variety of reasons why this has taken place, but I believe one of the main reasons is that children have been raised to go through the motions and not actually engage in the spiritual fight. On top of that, they haven't seen Mom and Dad madly in love with each other, and if this is all that Christianity is then they don't want anything to do with it.

Now is the time to quit playing church games and going through the motions. Our children deserve to see their parents be on fire for God and in love with each other and be dedicated to the spiritual fight. When our children see this, then they will want the same thing and they will begin to follow Jesus in a genuine way and begin to engage in the fight when they are young, not just when they get older. I don't believe that God wants to wait to use people when they are a certain age, but He desires to use them as soon as they're willing to be used.

When a family is united with Jesus and united as a family, then they are made strong in The Lord, develop spiritual grit, and can fight together against the enemy. As the children grow up and become adults, they will be more likely to follow the path that was laid before them by their faithful parents.

There's no stronger "corner" than a family, and when the family is devoted to God, then He will use them to fight the fight He's called them to!

Do you have FAMILY when you're against the ropes?

ROUND 3: FIGHT

As your spiritual GRIT is developed, you must decide whether to continue to FIGHT or give up in the spiritual fight.

FIGHT FOR YOUR LIFE

The Rocky movies are arguably some of the greatest movies of all time. Even if you don't agree, it's hard not to think about some of the famous scenes from the series like Rocky fighting Apollo Creed, Mr. T, Draco, and perhaps the most famous scene of him running up the stairs and raising his hands high in the air once he reached the top. We love movies like this because we can relate to the grind it takes to keep going when life has us down, and Sylvester Stallone was no stranger to adversity himself. In the early 70s, he was an unknown actor trying to make it in New York, and after having some success, he was still broke, and was trying to make it. Sylvester (Sly) describes that he got the idea for Rocky when he was watching an underdog fight the great Muhammad Ali.

"And then one night, I went out to see Muhammad Ali fight Chuck Wepner. And what I saw was extraordinary. I saw a man called 'The Bayonne Bleeder' fight the greatest fighter who ever lived. And for one brief moment, this supposed stumblebum turned out to be magnificent. And he lasted and knocked the champ down. I thought if this isn't a metaphor for life.[12]"

That was the catalyst for his idea: A man who was going to stand up to life, take a shot, and go the distance. He started writing and in three days, had the script done. It was only ninety pages, and only about a third of it was used in the movie, but it was done. He was auditioning for another role in a different movie, and he realized that he wasn't the right actor for the role. He made a bold decision and decided to show the producers the script that he wrote, and they loved it! The only problem, they didn't want to have Sylvester Stallone play the main character, Rocky. They even offered $360,000 for the script, with the condition that he wouldn't play Rocky. Sly had no car and

$106 to his name, but he believed in himself and knew he could do it, so he turned down their offer. The producers eventually caved and gave the role to him, and the rest is history.

Sylvester Stallone had to decide to give up or keep fighting for his dream, and his decision to keep fighting led to one of the most successful movie franchises ever. What if he decided to quit? What if he sold his dream? We wouldn't have the famous quotes coming from his unique personality and distinct accent. I believe the movie captured the hearts of the people because it resonated with the inner fighter inside each of us and because Rocky was fighting for his dream in real life. That's why quotes like this are being quoted still to this day:

"Let me tell you something you already know. The world ain't all sunshine and rainbows. It's a very mean and nasty place and I don't care how tough you are, it will beat you to your knees and keep you there permanently if you let it. You, me, or nobody is gonna hit as hard as life. But it ain't about how hard ya hit. It's about how hard you can get hit and keep moving forward. How much you can take and keep moving forward. That's how winning is done!" - Sylvester Stallone, *Rocky Balboa*.

Rocky is absolutely right. Life is going to hit us harder than anything else, but we must decide whether to keep on moving or not, even after we take the blow. This is the epitome of grit. When life knocks you down, do you stay down, or do you get back up? For Sly, he was fighting for his dream to become an actor even when others overlooked him. What about you? What are you fighting for? What's your dream? I would argue that most people aren't short of dreams, but they lack the grit to keep pursuing their dreams when things don't go their way. I love what Mike Tyson says (who was one of the most feared fighters of all time) when he was asked if he was nervous about his opponent's fight plan against him.

"Everyone has a plan until they get punched in the mouth." - Mike Tyson

Isn't that the truth? Most of us won't find ourselves in the boxing ring fighting some of the most dangerous fighters in the world, but all of us will find ourselves fighting, and our opponent is much more powerful than any professional fighter. Our opponent is Satan and ourselves. What do you do when you get knocked down by Satan's tactics? Do you surrender and decide it's not worth it to keep fighting in the spiritual fight? Do you give up your faith in God? When things don't go your way, do you choose to do what you want to do rather than what God wants you to do? See, your greatest opponent in the fight of life isn't other people (like we looked at earlier in this book), it's not even the obstacles that stand in the way of your dream (like Sly), it's Satan trying to "steal, kill, and destroy," and it's you choosing to follow your plans rather than God's.

When life punches you in the mouth and things don't go as planned, what is your response? Do you give up and throw in the towel? Or do you decide to get back up again and keep fighting? Remember, we are not strong enough to be victorious in this battle with our own strength and wisdom, but with God's help, we are strong enough! He will provide the strength, but we must be willing to keep on fighting and keep on trusting.

I believe we are living in one of the least resilient generations of all time[13]. I know I sound like an "old head" here, but I believe it. (As a pastor, I've found this to be true when counseling younger people and discovering the things that are normal to them, but not to my generation and others. I've watched people not hold down jobs, become overwhelmed with minimal weight on them, more indecisive, and more stressed than ever. I'm not pretending to be an expert and I'm not saying this is everyone, but I do see this in the younger generation more than I ever have before. I do believe that this generation is incredibly bright and is asking great questions, but I believe there's a resilience (grit) issue. Whether it's from the impact of technology, social media, or other things, what I do know is we can't continue to go down this route.

It's God's will that we are "Strong and immovable" (1 Corinthians 15:58). When we lose the ability to be strong, the trials of life become too much to bear, and I believe that's what we're seeing happen. While it's good to try and help our kids be in the best situations possible to ensure their health and safety, if it's taken too far, then our kids become spoiled, entitled, and soft. I'm not suggesting that everyone is weak and that we need to start showing "tough love" to our kids, but I am saying that when there's not enough tension on someone, then they will break at the first hint of pressure when it comes their way. Embrace the tension, rely on God, and grow stronger!

FIGHT THROUGH FAILURE

When you think of a warrior, who comes to mind? For me, I think of Maximus from *Gladiator*, or Leonidas from *300*. Both movies are based on fearless warriors who show a relentless amount of grit. I also love war movies that are based on the lives of real-life heroes that faithfully served their countries. They were committed to their country and did whatever it took to serve and protect, and many of them lost their lives doing so. There's something ingrained within us that loves watching people be so committed to something that they are willing to give their lives to it. This "warrior mentality" doesn't only apply to physical warfare, it even applies to our favorite athletes, musicians, entrepreneurs, etc. When we hear about the dedication some of the greats put into developing their craft, it causes us to be in awe of the fact that they got to where they did, but we don't spend a lot of time focusing on how they got there.

Both in the movies and in real life, the greatest "warriors" in their field often rose from great adversity and committed their lives to developing their craft to become great. These people that we look up to didn't wake up one day and suddenly become great. They put the work in each day. This creates grit and helps them to keep persevering to get to where they want to be. Many of them failed time and time again, but they were determined to not let their failure prevent them from continuing to fight.

Michael Jordan is arguably the greatest basketball player that's ever lived, but even he was cut from his high school basketball team. When asked about how he felt about this experience, he said, "Everybody goes through disappointments, it's how you overcome those disappointments. I just wasn't good enough. It was the best thing that could happen to me."[14] Not many people will end up being known as one of the greatest of all time in their field, but we can all become great by refusing to allow setbacks to prevent us from continuing to fight. The things that we admire about Michael Jordan, Tom Brady, Tiger Woods, Serena Williams, Michael Phelps, and other greats (sorry for only using sports examples) are their skills and accomplishments, and also, their sheer grit to keep pushing forward. No one likes setbacks, but setbacks can be what propels us forward and motivates us to work harder than ever before.

Many of us have sought to be great men and women of God, but through the trials and setbacks in life, we have found ourselves feeling like spiritual failures rather than champions. It's incredibly discouraging to feel like we've wasted years of our lives trying to figure out what God wants us to do and after all, the things we have done haven't been that successful anyway. Does this sound familiar? Sometimes, life is just hard and discouraging, even when there's nothing too devastating going on.

I don't know about you or not, but for me, I've had seasons in my spiritual journey that were "good" on the outside, but they didn't seem good on the inside. Call it seasonal depression, temporary sadness, or whatever you want, but sometimes, I just think some times are harder than others. I think the Psalms are a great place to camp out during these seasons because they remind us to praise God for who He is and all that He's done. It's important to give God thanks even when we don't feel thankful. I believe part of our spiritual formation is learning not to rely too heavily on our emotions and rely on the strength of God to sustain us through the hard seasons.

I say this because sometimes the greatest fight that you and I will ever have is continuing to push through mental and emotional battles. We have covered a great deal of the spiritual and physical battle, but the emotional and mental one can be just as hard at times. The greatest athletes weren't free from these challenges, but they learned to endure through them. As Christians, we too must learn to endure the spiritual fight when it comes to these areas.

This is why Paul often speaks about putting our minds on Christ, as well as casting our worries and anxieties on Him (2 Corinthians 10:5-6). Can you imagine the mental and emotional fight that Paul had to endure after being repeatedly persecuted, threatened, and beaten? How does someone who goes through what he did have the ability to say, "rejoice always" (1 Thessalonians 5:16-18)? It's because he prayed to God continuously and trusted God would give him the strength he needed.

Paul not only developed the spiritual and physical grit he needed to endure, but also the mental and emotional grit. There had to have been times that he felt like he was in a "dark night of the soul" season and didn't feel like he was doing enough or didn't measure up. Perhaps when he was chained up in prison, different thoughts of doubt and discouragement came over him because he couldn't see what the other churches were doing. I know that's hard to imagine, but he's human, so I believe he did. The only way he was able to keep fighting was to trust that he did all that he could, and trusted God with the rest.

I can't imagine the stress that Paul felt with all that he did and all that he went through, but I know how much stress I had when I helped plant our church.

I was twenty-three years old when I became the founding co-pastor of our church, and nothing could have prepared me for knowing how to manage the pressure of leading a fast-growing church. Our church grew very quickly, and we got to see incredible things happen, but this pace of ministry wasn't something I could grow into; it literally happened overnight. With me being so young, newly married, just planting the church, going to school, and additional dysfunctional family situations, I didn't know how to go about it all, so I just kept grinding in my own strength. I had a solid relationship with God, but I wasn't resting in Him and letting the Spirit help guide me and give me the wisdom I needed. I didn't have a good understanding of having healthy rhythms, and the more pressure I felt, the more I tried to "dig deep" and keep moving forward, just like I always had before, but then something happened to me that I hadn't ever experienced.

I got up to preach in our first of three services one Sunday morning, and everything seemed normal, until it wasn't. As I worked my way through my sermon, I began to preach about Jacob and Esau, and then suddenly I felt like I was about to pass out. I couldn't remember anything that I had studied all that week, and I couldn't even remember the plot of one of the most well-known stories in the Bible! I tried to play it off by smiling and telling the church that I didn't feel good, and I took a step back and chugged an entire water. I'm sure people were thinking I relapsed and was high! I confidently stood back in the center of the stage and then everything was pretty much a blur from that point on. I remember looking at some confused faces in the crowd and I felt like my heart was coming out of my chest.

I looked at my co-pastor (God-mom) and held up the microphone and said, "You're up." Bless her heart! She hadn't even looked at the sermon that week and had to step up and preach my sermon. She's incredible. I ran to the bathroom and was followed by nurses that attended our church and they asked me a series of questions and eventually decided it was best that I went to urgent care. Once I got to urgent care, they sent me to the emergency room. From there, they did a variety of tests and gave me an MRI due to my health record, and after hours and hours of this, they concluded, "You had an anxiety attack. Your pace right now caught up with you."

I wanted to punch the doctor when he said that. I didn't say anything to him, but I was thinking to myself, 'Anxiety? If you knew my story you would know that this is nothing. Clearly, you don't know how to do your job and you're simply wrong.' I had heard of this before, but to be honest, I kind of rolled my eyes and dismissed it. Not that I didn't think it was real, but I just didn't understand it. Now, here I was, in one of the most embarrassing moments of my life, and the doctor was telling me that I was one of those people who struggled with anxiety. I was in disbelief.

I left that day and I didn't want to talk to anyone, and I wanted to escape. I had no idea what this looked like for me going forward and I didn't know if this would immediately leave me or if it was something I would live with for the rest of my life. The "fearless" leader was now afraid, and I wasn't sure if I would ever bounce back. Sounds dramatic I know, but it shook me to the core.

A week later, I found myself preaching at a youth conference for the first time since my embarrassing "run off the stage" moment. I was terrified, and I wanted to get out of this situation, but I couldn't. Madi was in the car with me before we went in, and she could tell I was panicking, so she prayed over me and told me I had this. I smiled and pretended like I was fine, but I knew I wasn't. By the time I got up to preach, the same feeling that I had before came over me again, but I was determined to keep going. I would love to tell you that when I began to preach it was the most Holy moment I'd ever experienced, and hundreds of people got saved and the panic left me—but that's not what happened.

I struggled the whole time. I was fighting back panic and I wanted to run away again, but I didn't. After the worst thirty minutes of my life, I went directly to the car and felt like crying like a baby. Madi eventually made it to the car and was trying to figure out how I was doing, and she could tell by my demeanor that I wasn't doing good.

"I'm never preaching again," I said.

She looked at me with a scared look on her face, but she was trying to be the calm, supportive wife at the same time, so she had a fake smile on her face. I'm sure what she was thinking was, 'Umm babe, you're not good at anything else, so you're going to have to figure this out!' Not really. Instead, she grabbed my hand and affirmed to me that I was going to be okay and that she would be with me as we walked it out together. Though I was scared (and she probably was as well), it gave me peace knowing I wasn't alone. I wasn't sure how I was going to preach again, and I didn't even want to attempt to do it, but I knew God was with me.

After a couple of weeks of not preaching, my anxiety would come and go periodically, and I wasn't ready to return to preaching yet. One Sunday, I was worshiping in the front row and the worship team started singing the song "This Is How I Fight My Battles," by Upper Room. When I saw the lyrics, "It may look like I'm surrounded, but I'm surrounded by You," I immediately began to weep, and I fell to my knees and lifted my hands high into the air and cried out to God for help. I felt the presence of God unlike I'd felt in a very long time, and I knew in that moment that God was stronger than anything I was facing. God revealed to me in that moment that I had been relying on my own strength and though I was used to trials, this was a different type than I'd ever experienced before. My grit had been developed in other areas, but not in this new season. I had been a "fighter" my entire life due to life circumstances, so I was used to persevering through trials, but I had met my match. I couldn't defeat this on my own, and I was truly *against the ropes.*

This season taught me how to rely on God and adopt healthy rhythms in a way that I hadn't before. I slowed down, learned to say no, honored the sabbath, put my wife before others, got wise counsel, and allowed the Spirit to strengthen me. This was a process (and still is), but I was able to get back to preaching again, and I've never had to quit preaching again during a sermon (praise God). There were still some scares at times, but I developed spiritual grit and recognized when the anxiety was coming, and I was able to attack it. Rather than letting it just attack me, I attacked back by praying, reading God's Word, listening to worship, walking (sounds crazy, but it helped), and understanding why I was feeling the way I was.

As I look back on this, I still hate to think about it, but I'm thankful for it. I wouldn't want to go through it again, but I know I'm stronger because of it. I've been able to empathize with others who struggle with it and help them learn to attack it when it comes, rather than giving in to it. I'm aware that everyone is different, and this impacts everyone differently. I don't want to pretend to have all the answers when it comes to it, but I do believe God allowed me to go through it to strengthen me, but also to help strengthen others.

Anxiety is running rampant in our world, and as a pastor, I've watched countless Christians be so paralyzed by it that it's become their identity in some cases. I believe our society has overcompensated with it, we've accepted defeat in this area, and I believe it's a spiritual attack. Hear me out, it's certainly real and it's terrible, but I believe that God gives us the ability to be free from it or, at least be strong through it. Everyone's experience is different, but I'm afraid that too many people are trusting doctors, medication, psychologists, books, etc., rather than God. These things can absolutely help people! However, we need to ask the question if we've invited the Holy Spirit in this process and if we've allowed Him to strengthen us in our spiritual journey. God will give us everything we need to persevere, and He's never going to tell us to do something without giving us the ability to do it (through His strength). If we're commanded to be "anxious in nothing" (Philippians 4:6), it's because God believes we don't have to be anxious. Before you discount this and skip over it, ask yourself if you believe that God can give you this ability. Paul certainly did, and he had more to be anxious about than all of us!

The way we're able to do this is through prayer and thankfulness.

"6 Don't worry about anything; instead, pray about everything. Tell God what you need and thank him for all he has done. 7 Then you will experience God's peace, which exceeds anything we can understand. His peace will guard your hearts and minds as you live in Christ Jesus" (Philippians 4:6-7 NLT).

As we pray and allow the Holy Spirit to guide us, and as we thank God for His strength, he "guards our hearts and minds" from the attacks of anxiety. I believe God wants to free us from this, but we have to rely on Him in a way that we never have before. Keep praying, keep trusting, keep fighting.

When I find myself feeling low mentally and emotionally, I read scriptures to remind myself that God will give me the strength to continue to go on. If we don't give up, we will watch God not only bring us through our lowest seasons, but we will come out stronger on the other side. Grit typically comes from pain, and God will use that pain to make us stronger. Great athletes intentionally put themselves through vigorous pain in their training so they can push through the pain when it counts the most. I'm not saying God always causes the pain that we go through, but He will allow us to go through it at times to strengthen us and comfort us.

Maybe you feel like you've failed too many times or feel like a failure altogether, but I promise you that's not true. Remember, it's not how many times you fall, but how many times you get up. Maybe you find yourself repeatedly falling back into the same dark season and you feel like there's no way out, and that's just the way it will always be. If that's you, let the verse below encourage you!

"For though the righteous fall seven times, they rise again" (Proverbs 24:16 NIV).

Those who are in Christ will always rise again because we share in His resurrecting power! If we don't quit, then God will help us back up and we will continue to keep fighting. Even if you had a failure this doesn't mean that you are a failure. If you've failed to be where you want to be, then just keep relying on God. Even when you don't think you'll ever feel peace and joy again, I know you will, if you don't quit.

Keep praying, keep believing, keep fighting, and I believe you will find yourself stronger than you've ever been and realize God got you through it all!

FIGHT FOR GREATNESS

Dictionary.com defines greatness as, "the quality or state of being important, notable, or distinguished."[15] We live in a world that desires us to be great by being important to others, and this is exhausting and temporary. No matter how great you might be, the moment you are no longer at your peak, you are irrelevant. You might still have wealth and fame in some areas, but the world is going to move on without you, whether you like it or not. Again, I'm not trying to be a downer, there's good news coming!

As much as I love a good movie like *Rocky* or watching a documentary like *The Last Dance* (about Michael Jordan), something is missing in these great stories, and that's because they are incomplete. They aren't incomplete because they didn't excel like they should have, but because their success (in the world's eyes) is temporary. I'm not saying this referring to their statistics eventually being broken (though this might happen), but to point out that all things will eventually disappear if they are not rooted in God's Word.

Jesus said, "Heaven and earth will pass away, but my words will not pass away" (Matthew 24:35).

Personally, I think that God enjoys watching His creations learn to push themselves to accomplish things that the world has never seen before because it shows off His creation. This isn't diminishing these athletes' incredible dedication and determination, in fact, people can honor God with their God-given talent by glorifying Him with the platform that they've been given. When someone brings honor to God and desires to put Him at the center of everything they do, then what they do for God will have an eternal reward.

Colossians 3:23-24 NTL says, "Work willingly at whatever you do, as though you were working for the Lord rather than for people. Remember that the Lord will give you an inheritance as your reward and that the Master you are serving is Christ."

This is what true greatness looks like, doing whatever you do as if it were for the Lord, not for yourself or others. This is why all the other accomplishments are incomplete because they have a me-centered focus rather than being God-centered. When you're focused on yourself, you can never be great in God's eyes because you lived for yourself rather than for God and others, and you won't get a reward in Heaven for things like this.

This is good news for the average person (like me) because this levels the playing field for everyone. If the only way you can be great is to be famous in the world's eyes by accomplishing certain accolades that fit the criteria of what is impressive to others, then most of us are failures. But this isn't the case!

If greatness signifies importance, then those who live for God are considered great because we are important to God! The scriptures are filled with promises of God's love for us (John 3:16), and when we know we are loved by Him, we are then freed of the temptation to be validated by others based on our performance. It's when we grasp God's love (with our limited understanding) that we can also live for God by giving Him our all in both our pursuit of becoming more like Him (Philippians 2:5), and by working for Him in our daily responsibilities such as being a wife, mother, teacher, board member, etc.

This is what Paul meant when he says to work for the Lord rather than man (Colossians 3:23-24). We must take the responsibilities that we have seriously and believe that God has us there for a purpose and a reason, and we need to fight for our purpose in our different roles. I believe that God wants to use His Church (the people) to witness to the world around them by living Godly lives, but I also believe God desires to see Christians be just as committed to their roles as the famous people that we look up to. Not in a way that detracts us from our faith or takes us away from being the leader in our families, but a healthy and focused approach that desires to do the very best they can do with where they are at. This is what it looks like to fight the daily fight in your life. This is what it means to be great, to live for God by giving Him your heart and giving Him everything else. When we have this mindset, we wake up every day chasing greatness in a way that has eternal value, not temporary value.

Every sport has a Hall of Fame (again, sorry for the sports references, but you get the point), and it's a place that reflects on the greatness of those who've gone before us. The Bible symbolizes the Hall of Fame for those who followed God before us. In Hebrews 11, there is a long list of names of those who displayed great faith throughout the Old Testament and their names appear in this passage to remind us that we share in the same faith that they had, except now we have the fulfillment of Jesus. How amazing is it that we get to carry on the greatness that they had by putting our faith in God, just like they did? We might not see the same things they saw, but we might experience things they didn't see.

That's not the point. The point is that they were dedicated to keeping their faith strong in God, no matter how hard it got. The encouraging part is that they were flawed and made mistakes just like us. How often do we convince ourselves that we are too average, too broken, too young, too old, too busy, etc.? When we fall into these temptations, we will justify our actions by telling ourselves or others that we would do more for God, but we just can't.

"But hey, I could be doing worse, right?"

Every time I hear an excuse like this it saddens me, not because I judge the person and shame them because I think they should be doing more, but because I understand that they have been deceived by the enemy or they have lost the fight in them. This can happen for a multitude of reasons, but at the center of it is that he/she is not fighting the spiritual fight the way that God desires. People often get discouraged because he/she sees what others are doing and feel like they aren't doing enough themselves, so they end up not doing anything different. God created you to be you, not someone else! (Psalm 139:13-14).

You might be thinking, "Wait, I thought you just told me that I needed to do more, but now you're telling me not to be like others who are actually doing more?" Let me break it down further. God absolutely wants you to be comfortable in your unique self, but the best version of yourself, and that's being who He's called you to be and doing what He's called you to do. We can get discouraged when we feel like we aren't as gifted as others or aren't doing as much as them, but these are lies from the enemy, and he knows that if he can keep you from believing that God wants to use you, then he doesn't have to worry about you fighting back. However, as you grow into a healthy understanding of your identity, you will begin to desire to fight for your calling and want to get back up and keep moving forward.

This is when we can allow what God is doing in other people's lives to motivate us rather than discourage us. When we are healthy in our understanding of our purpose and calling, we can then appreciate what God's doing in others and we can be motivated to fight just as hard in our spiritual fight. We are meant to be great according to God's standards (not the world's), but we must fight for it. Whatever you feel God leading you to do, give it your everything, work for Him, not the approval of others, work to be great in whatever you do, and don't lose your fight!

FIGHT LIKE A SPIRITUAL WARRIOR

When you think of "warriors" in the Bible, who comes to mind? People often think of Joshua, Caleb, Samson, and certainly David, and these are certainly warriors that were used by God mightily. However, a spiritual warrior isn't just one that is involved in a physical war, but also spiritual.

Webster defines Warrior as, "A person engaged or experienced in warfare."

In the spiritual sense, we can become a warrior by becoming experienced in fighting the enemy. The ultimate example of the "spiritual warrior" is Jesus Himself. Have you ever considered how Jesus was a warrior?

Though He was fully God, He was also fully man, and He had to choose to engage in the fight or not. He knew His mission, but it would require Him to keep pushing forward. If we're not careful, we can forget Jesus' humaneness and assume His crucifixion (and all the things leading up to it) didn't bother Him, but it did. He knew the pain of the crucifixion was going to be a lot, but He also knew the pain of Him taking on the sin of the world was going to be even harder. With all of this in mind, my mind goes to His journey to the cross while He had to carry it after being whipped and beaten.

"Carrying the cross by himself, he went to the place called Place of the Skull (in Hebrew, Golgotha). 18 There they nailed him to the cross" (John 19:17-18).

This would have been an excruciating process, but He kept pushing forward and showed the ultimate form of grit (physically and spiritually). After carrying the heavy cross on his back for many miles, He eventually was killed after being nailed to a cross. That's what our Savior did for us. Not only was He a warrior by going through everything He did physically, but He was a warrior spiritually by willingly dying on the cross for us. He could have gotten Himself off the cross easily, but instead, He sacrificed Himself. On top of that, He asks the Father to forgive the very people who killed Him.

This is what being a spiritual warrior looks like! A warrior isn't just one who's willing to take on a giant physically, but also one who is willing to do whatever it takes spiritually. It's not that these two aren't related, but as Christians, we wage war differently than the world wages war (2 Corinthians 10:3-4 NLT). This doesn't mean that there's never a physical battle alongside the spiritual one, I mean after all, when Jesus comes back to Earth, He's going to defeat Satan physically for good (Revelation 19). Many people have an image of Jesus only being a humble King who's willing to always turn the other cheek, but this isn't all that He is. He came as a humble baby, but He's coming back as a fierce King to judge the world. He rode on a donkey, but He's coming back on a white horse. Jesus is the ultimate warrior who is a warrior both physically and spiritually.

To end this section, I want to point out something that maybe you haven't realized before. Many people think of David (before he was a King) as a fierce warrior even before he killed Goliath because he had killed a lion and a bear (1 Samuel 17:34-36), and that would certainly qualify him as a warrior. I find two things very interesting about this.

First, there's no record of David being known as a warrior yet, and people didn't think he was capable of defeating Goliath because his brothers mocked him when he showed up on the battlefield and asked about Goliath. King Saul also told him that he was too little and too inexperienced. However, my question to them is, "How many bears or lions have you killed?" We know that some had (Benaiah in 2 Samuel), but it couldn't have been that common. My point is that David was as capable as any other person Israel had to attempt to kill Goliath based on his track record, but because he wasn't old enough in people's eyes and because he didn't have the influence yet, people disqualified him.

David most likely killed the lion and bear (oh my) when no one was around because he was only doing his job, which was to protect his sheep as a good shepherd. Even then, David knew he was able to defeat these fierce beasts only by God's strength. We know this because when he's giving his case to King Saul to let him fight Goliath he says, "The Lord who rescued me from the claws of the lion and the bear will rescue me from this Philistine!" (1 Samuel 17:37). David knew he was anointed to be King one day (1 Samuel 15), but he had to go back to the field and be a shepherd, and that didn't mean trials weren't going to come his way. In fact, I'd say a lion and a bear coming at you was a huge trial! However, he knew the calling God had for his life and he had to be courageous when the trials came his way, and when he was brave, God gave Him supernatural strength and ability, and he was quick to give God the credit.

This is why he was able to say with confidence (not cockiness, there's a difference) that God would deliver the Philistine to him. David had watched God move in the past and he believed He would do it again. God gave David spiritual grit by letting him take on bigger and bigger opponents, and this built his spiritual and physical grit. God might have anointed you for something, but it doesn't mean it's going to be easy, and it doesn't mean it'll be immediate. You must be brave every step of the way, and just like David, you must first be built up spiritually so that you will stay humble and know where your strength comes from. Then you must also be built up physically by taking on lions and bears before you face a giant. Like David, you might be mocked, laughed at, or overlooked, but that's okay, because we know that we live for the approval of God, not man. Face your giant!

The second thing I find fascinating is that David is quick to point out that Goliath not only called out Israel's army, but he focuses on the fact that it was God's army he was calling out. "For he has defied the armies of the living God!" (1 Samuel 17:36). This might not seem like a big thing at first, but it has a deep spiritual connection to it. David understood that this was not only a physical war, but also spiritual. David was shocked to find the entire nation of Israel paralyzed with fear when he walked up to the battle scene.

David wasn't seeing what everyone else was seeing. He obviously took notice of the giant that everyone else saw, but I don't believe he was just looking at the physical opponent, but the spiritual as well. I believe he saw Goliath as an opponent to the God of Israel, not just Israel itself. There's a difference.

When we only see the flesh and blood side of our opponents, we compare one another physically, but when we see the spiritual component of opposition, then we see things that can only be given by the Holy Spirit (Numbers 22:23-35, 2 Kings 6:17-20). David knew that Goliath's mockery of the nation of Israel was a direct attack on God Himself and it infuriated him. We must ask ourselves if we take the spiritual attacks against God personally as David did. If someone was disrespecting your earthly father relentlessly, I can guarantee you that you would eventually get tired of it and do something about it, regardless of your relationship with him. David had an intimate relationship with God, and it hurt him to hear someone defy God's people that way. Although we won't find ourselves in the same place as David, we will find ourselves in situations that cause us to do something about it, or cower down as the other soldiers did. This can look like a variety of things, but at its core, it's when we feel a spiritual battle going on in the form of physical opposition.

One example is when you feel the need to stand up for something that opposes our Christian faith, and you feel like you would be disobeying God if you didn't say or do something. With that being said, we must be very in tune with the Holy Spirit in these moments, because we can pick a battle with a "giant" that God never asked us to fight, and we can not only lose the battle, but also misrepresent God in the process. David was a man after God's own heart, so he was able to know when it was time to speak up and when it was time to go to war.

FIGHT THE FIGHT OF FAITH

If you've been in church long enough, you've most likely heard the expression "fight the good fight of faith." The apostle Paul wrote these words in a Roman prison to his spiritual son, Timothy, who was a young pastor at the church of Ephesus. Paul knew his life would most likely be coming to an end soon from the persecution he was facing due to his faith in Jesus. Timothy had followed Paul around before he became a pastor, and he knew how committed Paul was and he also knew how real the spiritual fight was. Many scholars believe that Timothy struggled with being timid (2 Timothy 1:7-8), and Paul encouraged Timothy to be strong and to keep fighting until the very end.

Paul understood that God had used him in a powerful way ever since Jesus visited him on Damascus Road in order to fight the spiritual darkness by spreading the Gospel through planting churches, preaching the Word, and performing miracles. With this came immense spiritual opposition as well as various trials (that I mentioned earlier), and yet while Paul is once again sitting in a prison cell, he's encouraging Timothy to fight the good fight. How is it that someone who has gone through as much as Paul has can have the audacity to say the fight is "good?" Like Jesus, I think we can read the Scriptures and assume that Paul was given such strength by God that it didn't bother him as much as it would us. This isn't true at all. It's true that God gave him strength, but not that it didn't bother him! He called the fight "good" because he knew this was the calling that God had called him to and because it had spiritual implications, not just physical. Paul knew there was more going on than just people being mad at him, and he was determined to keep fighting until the end.

Acts 9:15-16 NLT "15 But the Lord said, 'Go, for Saul is my chosen instrument to take my message to the Gentiles and to kings, as well as to the people of Israel. 16 And I will show him how much he must suffer for my name's sake.'"

Paul knew he had a calling, but he also knew there was a lot that came with that calling. I don't believe that God was punishing him for persecuting the church, but I do believe that God wanted to refocus his zeal and that it would require a lot of grit. As I mentioned earlier in this section, I believe we were meant for greatness, but this greatness comes with a great cost.

Following Jesus' plans for Paul was a complete surrender of His plans and a daily decision to keep fighting. This is why Paul can say, "Follow my example, as I follow the example of Christ" (1 Corinthians 11:1 NIV). He knew he not only talked the talk, but he walked the walk. This is why he could tell Timothy to keep on fighting the good fight. Paul knew that it was essential for Timothy to grow strong in the Lord and be a spiritual warrior as well, so that the Gospel could continue to spread. Paul also knew that if he wasn't dead yet, then God wasn't done yet.

GET TO FIGHTING!

I'm not sure there's another person in the Bible (besides Jesus) who understood the magnitude of what he was a part of than Paul. Very shortly after his conversion, he began preaching the good news of Jesus.

"And immediately he began preaching about Jesus in the synagogues, saying, "He is indeed the Son of God!" (Acts 9:20).

How does the person who goes from persecuting Christians immediately begin to preach? One who understands that God rescued him from the deception of the enemy. Paul used to persecute Christians not because he hated God, but because he thought he was serving God by "protecting" His church. This shows how easy it is for the enemy to deceive people. Paul (formally known as Saul) wasn't an uninformed rebel. He was a respected religious leader under the Jewish law. He knew the prophecies about the Messiah, but he didn't believe that Jesus was the Messiah. So, once he received the Holy Spirit, he knew that it was his responsibility to inform the other Jews (and Gentiles) that he was wrong, and that Jesus is in fact the Messiah.

Paul wasn't committed to sharing the Gospel just because he felt bad for what he did to others, but because he realized he was used for evil. When you discover you've been deceived and used by someone, it creates anger within you that makes you want to lash out and get revenge. This is what fueled Paul (I believe) to do what he did. He didn't want Satan to continue to deceive another person and he was willing to be anyone, do anything, and go anywhere that the Spirit wanted to "set the captives free."

This is why Paul's letters are filled with descriptions of the spiritual realm and the spiritual fight because he wanted others to understand what's really going on. Revenge on people is not of God, but I believe revenge on Satan is absolutely acceptable, and might I say recommended! Paul didn't wait to go to seminary before preaching the Gospel, in fact, he had already done that, and it prevented him from recognizing the Messiah. (For the record, I'm a supporter of higher education. I've certainly done it, but education itself can be a trap if you rely on knowledge more than the Spirit.) It's not how much you know about God, it's how much you actually know Him. He knew that he was commissioned by God to preach the Word and he wasn't going to let his past prevent him from moving forward.

This is why I could relate to Paul so much when I got saved because I had a tainted past, but I also had a calling to preach. I wrestled with feeling inferior to others when I felt the call to preach because I didn't come from the right family, I didn't have the right story, I didn't have the right apparel, and I certainly didn't have the right words to feel qualified. That's when I came across this passage.

"15 This is a trustworthy saying, and everyone should accept it: 'Christ Jesus came into the world to save sinners'—and I am the worst of them all. 16 But God had mercy on me so that Christ Jesus could use me as a prime example of his great patience with even the worst sinners. Then others will realize that they, too, can believe in him and receive eternal life" (1 Timothy 1:15-16 NLT).

Paul considered himself the "worst of sinners," not in a bragging way, but because he was ashamed of the way he persecuted the Church, and at that point, no one else had persecuted the Church as badly as him. Again, Paul knew that Jesus had shown him grace and mercy and his response wasn't just to accept forgiveness and play it safe, but to immediately get in the spiritual fight and push back the gates of hell.

If you've been deceived like Paul and have been an instrument for evil (by the way, we all have) and have received Christ's forgiveness, then you need to decide if you're going to get in the fight or not. Our conversion experience has been described as rescued from a fire (hell). It's also been said that when we share the Gospel message with others, we are a firefighter going into a burning building and rescuing others. I agree with both of these analogies, and I believe most Christians would also agree. If this is the case, then what do we do about the thoughts of those who don't share their faith with others? What about those who are not engaging in the spiritual fight and are just sitting on the sidelines, taking it easy while the others are fighting?

This type of thinking and behavior is like the fireman who's not committed to rescuing someone and doesn't think their life is worth saving. This way of thinking is like the soldier who is too worried about getting home safe and he/she isn't worried about the soldier next to them getting ambushed on both sides of them. Though we wouldn't agree with this verbally, our actions affirm it. I'm not trying to beat you up spiritually, in fact I've had to repent of my lack of desire to spread the Gospel at times as well, and it stuns me when I have to repent of this because when I first got saved, I couldn't stop telling anyone and everyone about the person that saved my life! I understand that it can be harder to stay as motivated about sharing your faith as you did at first, but it doesn't mean that this is acceptable. Just because it can be tempting, and many people stop sharing their faith doesn't mean it's what God desires. When we begin to justify our actions or try to warn the new believer that their "Jesus high" will calm down eventually, then we need to realize we're being deceived.

How selfish and hypocritical is it of me to preach on Sundays and not tell people about Jesus throughout the week? There's absolutely a reason for gathering on Sundays and preaching to the church body (and this can even be evangelistic), but the best form of sharing the Gospel is telling others about Jesus when we're living our daily lives at work, the gym, bank, restaurant, etc. This isn't just the pastor's job though, if that's the case, then we're seriously outnumbered. When we begin to share the Gospel with others, we are fighting against the enemy and we're helping people in a spiritual war that they aren't even aware of.

Though Paul wasn't one of Jesus' disciples, he certainly took Jesus' words (from the disciples) to heart and dedicated his life to fulfilling the Great Commission (Matthew 28:18-20). Paul knew his mission was to spread the gospel, and it's yours as well. Before you excuse yourself from this kind of mission by saying you're not called to do what Paul and other pastors and church planters have been, remind yourself that Paul was also a tentmaker. He made a living by making tents (Acts 18:3), but he made disciples at all times. Whether he was making tents, preaching, or traveling, Paul knew he was there to make disciples. Like Paul, we too are here to make disciples. Do we need to raise our families, work hard at our jobs, and take care of our responsibilities? Absolutely. However, when we make this the main thing, we have lost sight of the spiritual fight we're called to be in. If you've gotten sidetracked, that's okay, get back in the ring and keep fighting!

TRAINING IS OVER, IT'S FIGHT TIME

Paul knew that he was now in a real spiritual fight, and this is why he was so passionate about sharing the Gospel and confronting the enemy, because he saw people as if they were against the ropes spiritually, and they were.

In *Rocky IV*, Apollo Creed (who is now Rocky's friend) tragically dies in a match with the fierce fighter named Drago. Rocky watches his long-time opponent and friend die in his arms as the Olympic gold medalist and a boxing champion from the Soviet Union stands there in victory, staring down Creed's corner.[16] The boxing world was anxious about what Rocky would do. Rocky had accomplished everything that he needed to accomplish, and his fame was at the highest level, so he didn't have anything to prove, but he knew he had another fight in him. (I'm well aware this is a movie, but it's one of the greatest movies ever, so don't judge.)

Though Rocky had beaten fierce opponents before, none were as threatening as Drago. This would be Rocky's greatest test yet, and it would require grit he hadn't ever developed before. If you've seen the movie, you know what happens next. Rocky travels to Russia and begins to train the old-fashioned way and escapes the media and other distractions. To Rocky, this wasn't just a match, this was war. As you can imagine, Rocky defeats Drago. (If you haven't watched this then I encourage you to.)

The training scenes of this movie are some of the most beloved scenes because Rocky had to dig deep and find himself again. Rocky became Rocky not because he was the most gifted and qualified fighter, but because he was the opposite of that. He had to learn on the go, but it was his intensity that made him great. Over time, he became a little distracted with his new level of fame and his focus wasn't purely on boxing anymore; however, the passing of Apollo did something in him that brought that fire back again. If you're familiar with boxing (or really any sport), you know that when fighters reach the top, it's hard for them to stay there because they lose their itch to become the best. Meanwhile, someone who was just as hungry as you or even hungrier is right on your heels coming for you, and if you're not prepared, they are going to knock you off your throne.

I believe that Paul understood this principle because he was used to watching athletes perform in the Greek games.[17] This is why he often used athletic references to relate to the Gospel because it connected with his audience as well as brought the spiritual fight concept to life. He knew he was in a fight, but again, his opponent was more powerful than any other opponent in the world, and his reward had eternal value.

"24 Don't you realize that in a race everyone runs, but only one person gets the prize? So run to win! 25 All athletes are disciplined in their training. They do it to win a prize that will fade away, but we do it for an eternal prize. 26 So I run with purpose in every step. I am not just shadowboxing. 27 I discipline my body like an athlete, training it to do what it should. Otherwise, I fear that after preaching to others I myself might be disqualified" (1 Corinthians 9:24-27).

Paul was fully committed to winning his fight, and he wasn't competing against anyone else other than Satan (evil) and himself (sinful nature). However, he was aware of his commitment to working hard for the Gospel because he points out that he worked harder than any of the other apostles (Holy flex, 1 Corinthians 15:10). He knew this wasn't pretend, which is why the New Living Translation (NLT) uses the term "shadow boxing," which is "to box with an imaginary opponent, especially as a form of training."[18] This helps the fighter see his/her strengths and weaknesses as well as gets them familiar with the fundamentals of fighting. This is a helpful tool in training, but it's only preparation for the real fight. The fighter knows that eventually, they will square off with a real fighter that will fight back. Bible studies, prayer groups, worship services, and other things like these are amazing (and helpful), but this is not all there is to being a Christian. To be a Christian (literally a Christ-follower) means that we follow Christ's example, and it's impossible to follow His example without engaging in spiritual warfare. Paul is telling us that we are no longer in training, the bell has rung and it's time to fight!

FIGHT YOUR FLESH

One of the toughest opponents you will have is yourself, and this is especially true when it comes to our temptations. While many blame Satan for indulging in sin, we oftentimes give him too much credit. Satan is the origin of evil, which is where sin comes from, but we also have our "flesh" or "sinful nature" that we inherited from Adam and Eve after they sinned. While it's true when we say our temptations are rooted in him, it's often a result of our own sinful nature that comes from within (James 1:14). The enemy can tempt us, though it's not likely to be Satan himself, but rather one of his demons since he can only be in one place at a time since he's not omnipresent like God. Often, we are our worst problem because we feed our flesh. What we feed grows, but what we starve dies, and too many of us feed our flesh and we lose the war with ourselves. As we continue to feed our flesh, this is where the enemy can come in and wreak havoc in our lives because we've opened the door for him to come in.

Paul gives us a long list of sins that come from our flesh (Galatians 5), but he also tells us that if we follow the Holy Spirit then we don't have to give in to temptations. He goes on to say that "these two forces are constantly fighting each other, so you are not free to carry out your good intentions." Whether you like it or not, you are in a constant fight with your flesh, and the only way to win is by the power of the Holy Spirit. The problem here is that many people think they are in the middle and don't do too much bad or too much good, just somewhere in between, but this is completely false. If you aren't growing closer to God then you are growing further away, there's no in-between. We must accept this reality and realize the way that our flesh is tempted.

For some, the negative consequences from giving into temptations are in the public's eyes and people can easily see they are sinful. Other temptations aren't public ones, and these can be dangerous because no one would ever know if they kept doing them. On the other hand, there are public consequences of temptations from one's life that aren't regarded as "sins" because they are socially acceptable. I'm not going to list any here because I don't want to focus on some more than others but read the Bible and see if there are things that you've regarded as "fine" that God actually calls "sin." At the root of them all is idolatry, which is anything that we put before God.

Let me pick on myself and say I've done this way more than I like to admit! This doesn't mean we throw up our hands in defeat and give way to what our sinful nature craves, no! Instead, we declare war and continue to fight spiritually and learn to rely on the Holy Spirit more and more until there's victory in an area. Let me just say, that just because you don't struggle with something doesn't mean you won't, or just because you don't struggle with something any longer doesn't mean the temptation can't come back. This is why Paul says, "If you think you are standing strong, be careful not to fall" (1 Corinthians 10:12). People often fall not because they "randomly" fell into sin one day as if a sign popped up out of nowhere and they ran into it. People ran into the sign because they weren't paying attention as they were walking, and as they got closer to the sign, it was too late.

We must be aware of what tempts us because if we don't know how we tick, then we are extremely vulnerable. If you read this and think to yourself, "I'm not tempted by anything," then let me let you know what your temptation is: PRIDE. If Jesus was tempted, we will be tempted, but we don't have to be slaves to it. I believe that the Holy Spirit can transform us into His image (2 Corinthians 3:18), and we can let God's spirit make us completely new, but it still takes grit to fight the urges. As amazing of a man of God as Paul was, he was still human and struggled just like we do (Romans 7:19). He knew perfection is possible only on the other side of Earth (Philippians 3), but he didn't let this discourage him or allow it to be an excuse to not keep growing in God, but instead he kept growing in his faith.

He also didn't allow it to prevent him from preaching boldly and doing the work that he knew God had called him to do. He understood that Satan wanted him to let shame paralyze him so that he wouldn't talk about the forgiveness of Jesus anymore. However, Paul was motivated even more to tell people about the forgiveness of Jesus because he wanted them to experience what he had. Paul had a choice to make every day just like you and me. Does he keep fighting or does he throw in the towel? He chose to keep fighting and God did great things through him, but he was just a man like you and me. Great things happen when we choose not to quit!

I believe one of Paul's greatest temptations isn't what we would initially think such as lust, lying, bitterness, etc., but rather the temptation to get spiritually lazy. I don't have any theological backing for this, I just am thinking practically. To do as much as he did in the amount of time he did, the temptation to get lazy would have had to be there at times. Possibly not, but if I were him, I could find myself thinking I deserve a break for a while.

Since Paul was such a strong leader for Jesus, I'm sure Satan (himself) did whisper to him at times, trying to convince him to quit. Satan probably wanted Paul to feel sorry for himself for how hard life was and just take it easy and call it quits. After all, Paul had worked so hard, he deserved to take it easy and retire early and ride off in the sunset, right? Not at all, it was the opposite! He knew he was here still to keep on fighting against the enemy. In fact, he struggled with wanting to go be with Jesus because it would be so much better for him, but he knew he still had work to do.

"21 For to me, living means living for Christ and dying is even better. 22 But if I live, I can do more fruitful work for Christ. So, I really don't know which is better. 23 I'm torn between two desires: I long to go and be with Christ, which would be far better for me. 24 But for your sakes, it is better that I continue to live" (Philippians 1:21-24 NLT).

Paul knew his ultimate home was to be with Jesus, so He didn't try to make Earth his comfy home where he could just sit back and relax until he died. No, he wanted to live for Jesus by giving His life to Him and continue to keep fighting even when it would be tempting to take it easy. This doesn't mean that he didn't rest or didn't enjoy the pleasures of the world, but he knew they weren't the main thing. This is why so much of his writings encourage Christians to keep going because he knew it was a temptation for people to become idle. While I'm not encouraging the "I will sleep when I'm dead" mentality that emphasizes hard work with no rest (that's another issue), I do think there's a temptation for many well-meaning Christians that get lazy in their spiritual walk and allow things to consume their time and energy. When we don't direct our attention to the spiritual fight that Jesus desires us to focus on, then we will spend our time focusing on lesser things and adopt worldly thinking patterns that aren't centered on God's plans.

"Yet we hear that some of you are living idle lives, refusing to work and meddling in other people's business" (2 Thessalonians 3:11 NLT).

Paul understood that if Christians don't engage in their spiritual fight, then they will become spiritually idle. Here, people were expecting Jesus to come back, and they quit carrying out their responsibilities and became lazy gossipers, but for others, it's being busy with their jobs and other things that lead to being spiritually lazy. Do you need to take care of your family and work hard at your job? Absolutely! However, you can become spiritually distracted in your busyness that you don't realize the enemy is distracting you from your main responsibility, which is to live your life for the glory of God and look to take back ground from the enemy at all times and in all places.

If you work hard at your job and become a respected worker who makes a lot of money but fails to witness to others while you're there, then you've missed it. If I preach a bunch of sermons and never talk to the guys at the gym about Jesus, then I've missed it. Everywhere we go we're looking to proclaim the Good News (Gospel) of Jesus to take ground back from the enemy in their lives. When we choose to become idle spiritually, we are deciding that our comfort is more important than God's calling in our lives.

I believe the greatest temptation that many Christians fall into without even realizing it is the temptation of spiritual laziness. By this, I mean

Christians who have received salvation, they are aware that God changed them, but they want to be as comfortable as possible. Not too bad, not too good, just right in the middle, but this is a trap. As Sir Isaac Newton once said, "A body at motion stays in motion; a body at rest stays at rest." If we stop fighting in the spiritual fight for too long, we will adopt a mentality that thinks "this is all there is to do," but that's not true. Once we see someone else doing something different than us, we have a decision to accept or reject that behavior.

I can desire to do something all day long and watch people on the internet do the thing I'm interested in, but until I actually do it, I will be fine with my current behavior. The same applies spiritually! We can be inspired by other men and women in their pursuit of God, but until we do something different, we will continue to get the same result. This is why Paul urged Christians to keep using their spiritual gifts because if not, they would dry up and people would forget they ever even had them. Like a muscle, if we don't exercise our faith, then it will weaken.

Don't coast through life "living the American dream," fight "with purpose" every day. Starve the flesh, feed the spirit, win the fight!

FIGHT TILL THE END

Every top ranked fighter worked their way up the ranks by facing tougher opponents along the way. Not only do their opponents get tougher, but so does the length of the fight as well. The longer the fight is, the harder it is for the fighter to keep going strong. Whenever fighters are training, they know how many rounds he/she is training for. Precisely how many rounds a contest is scheduled for depends on the situation. These days, most bouts last as little as four rounds and as many as twelve.

The fighters put in so much blood, sweat, and tears in training and work up to fight on the biggest stage if they are fortunate enough to. Little by little they built up the endurance to go another round. And another round. And another round. Suddenly, they are fighting twelve rounds, and they might have started with four. This might not seem like a big deal to you or me, but when you watch a top-notch athlete's struggle to stand and continue to fight after several rounds, I think we can agree it requires an incredible amount of grit to keep going.

In the same way (spiritually speaking), I believe that God builds our spiritual endurance along the way without us knowing we're getting stronger. We've looked a lot at Paul in this section, and we will continue to, because I believe he was the ultimate spiritual fighter, and I believe he modeled the endurance to fight until the final bell rang.

In Acts 14, Paul experiences whiplash (in every way). He and Barnabas go to Lystra and God uses Paul to heal a man that's been crippled since birth, and the whole city begins to worship them as if they were gods. Immediately after this, some Jews won the crowd (that was just praising them) over to their side and decided to try and kill them. I want to pause there and point out how fast things can change. One moment they are praised by the people and the next they are being attacked. Do you see the parallel with Jesus here? People praised Him one week and killed Him the next. There will be times when people will be excited about your faith and want to talk to you about it, and before you know it, you're being criticized for it. Again, following Jesus is not about the approval of others but of God alone. If you choose to live for the approval of man, then you will eventually be let down. Paul didn't let the praise of others get to his head because he knew it was God who healed the man, not him.

There's a temptation at times, to live for the social media likes to feel validated and accepted, but this leads to disaster. As Christians, we live the way that we do because of our love for Him, not the affirmation of others. It's not bad to enjoy the acceptance of others, but if this becomes your main motivation for living for Jesus, then you've missed the whole point of what it means to follow Him. We fight the fight God has called us to because we know we're there to spread His Word, not build our own reputation and platform. If we live for the approval of others, we will get distracted from why we were there in the first place. On top of that, I believe we will lose the anointing as well as the strength to continue to keep fighting. The opposite is true as well. When we are in the fight for the right reasons, we will experience a strength from God that we've never felt before, and we can continue to persevere through what He's assigned us.

One more thing to point out, notice that the Jews attacked him right after a miraculous healing. Jealousy can pop up when you appear to be "successful" to others, as well as spiritual attacks from the enemy. Many pastors have agreed that their biggest attacks normally come after their greatest victories. Why do you think this is? Because the enemy hates this and wants to interfere with God's plans, and that's when we must be strong in the Lord and keep fighting.

Look at what Paul does after getting attacked.

"19 Then some Jews arrived from Antioch and Iconium and won the crowds to their side. They stoned Paul and dragged him out of town, thinking he was dead. 20 But as the believers gathered around him, he got up and went back into the town" (Acts 19:19-20 NLT).

I say this often, but this is truly my favorite (or second favorite) passage of Scripture! Not even Rocky can compare to the sheer grit that Paul shows here! Let's empathize with Paul in this moment. Most people that I know have no real understanding of what it's like to be physically persecuted for their faith in Jesus. No one enjoys being yelled at, and here an entire town is yelling at Paul. As if that's not enough, he then gets stoned and drug out of town. The people thought he had had enough, and they silenced him forever.

At this moment, Paul had a choice. Do I stay down, or do I get back up? Paul had experienced a lot of trials up to this point, and he could have decided to call it quits. I mean, after all, he didn't sign up for this, right? Preaching is one thing, but getting beaten like this is another. Paul had a choice to make. The people must have thought to themselves that there was no way he could possibly get up from something like this, so they all turned back to go into the city. They had no idea that Paul wasn't dead, in fact, he was very much alive! I'm not sure what was going through his head at that moment, but what I do know is what happened next.

All that was left was Paul and the other Christian believers. I think this is important to point out because it demonstrates the power of family (like we looked at earlier). I'm sure Paul was already determined not to give up, but let's say he had. Can you imagine the looks on the faces of the people looking at him on the ground? He was their leader, their hero, and here he was on the ground, motionless. As his eyes began to open, he looked around and saw them looking at him. Like a fighter on the mat after getting knocked down, his head is spinning, and his hearing is going in and out. In the background, he hears the ref counting to ten before the fight is over and he's been TKO'd.

I like to think that he had a moment of thinking of all the things that God had allowed him to do so far as well as dreaming about what He had in store for his future. Once again, he looks up at the faces looking at him and he begins to move. The people are in awe. Surely not. There's no way he can possibly get up from this. I believe in this moment that Paul decided to put his faith in God even when it appeared like he was out of the fight. He had developed such great grit over the years, and he decided that this was not his last fight. He decided that if he wasn't dead, then God wasn't done!

Not only do we see his FAITH demonstrated, but we see the FAMILY of God come around him. Look at what it says, "as the believers gathered around him, he got up." Paul didn't get up from the ground until the believers gathered around him. This is a powerful representation of why it's so important to have people help you in your spiritual walk. Paul was as strong as anyone there's ever been when it comes to their spiritual grit, but even he needed people to help him up.

They not only helped him up physically, but I believe in every area of his life. I believe their presence gave him the comfort that he needed to know that he wasn't alone. When the people who were just praising him left after being swayed by Jews, he had to feel some abandonment. However, it was the true believers, not just those who are fans of Jesus and His power, who were there when he needed it the most. Their presence gave him the ability to get back up. This should challenge us (as the Church) to ask ourselves if we do this with others.

Like I said earlier, we were never meant to do life alone, especially in our spiritual walk. This is why it breaks my heart to talk to those who believe they don't need to attend church to be a Christian. Is this the right question to ask? I don't believe so, and I don't believe you can be a Christian and not desire to come alongside other believers and help them, because our love for others proves that we're His disciples (John 13:34-35). Scripture also teaches us that we can help others and others can help us when we face troubles, and this is exactly what happened here with Paul. He helped countless others before this and then once he was in need, they helped him.

A quick plug for pastors and leaders. Don't assume your pastor doesn't need help and encouragement. It's exhausting to carry out the responsibilities of a church along with carrying the weight of a lot of people's baggage. It's an honor to do this and I'm certainly not complaining, but I do know it can be easy to take leaders for granted, but they are human just like you and need encouragement as well. Also, if you're a pastor or leader, you need to humble yourself and be willing to receive help from those around you, rather than trying to do it all on your own. It's a two-way street. If the great apostle Paul needed family, we all need it!

The last part of this passage is my favorite, though. After Paul had faith and family, he also had FIGHT! It says, "he got up and went back into the town." Is there a more "bad to the bone" statement than this?! This is what Hollywood movies are based on, but this is real life. After Paul had been beaten to the point that the people thought he was dead, Paul had the audacity to "get back up" and go back to the same place he came from. This is crazy! Who does this type of thing?

Can you imagine what some of the believers around him were thinking when he walked back towards the town? "Paul, what are you doing? You're going the wrong way, you're not aware of where you're going, you're not thinking clearly!" The thing is, Paul knew exactly what he was doing. He knew that if God had spared his life, then He wasn't going to allow him to die now. Like I've said, people think because it's Paul that he was fine and it wasn't hard for him physically and spiritually to keep going, but this is not true. Paul was most likely bruised, cut, and bloody to the point where he was unrecognizable. This wasn't his camouflage tactic, because people would have noticed that he was the man they just stoned. Paul was able to get up and go in because he had the spiritual grit to press on, even when everyone around him most likely wanted him to quit, but he knew his fight wasn't over.

You and I might not be in the same position as Paul, but we have been and will continue to be faced with a decision where our fight is put to the test in a grueling way. Many of you have already been faced with this decision in a variety of different ways, and you're still fighting. I don't wish this on anyone, but most likely there are more battles ahead that will test your grit once again. It's important to remind you that when I say grit, I'm not referring to your own personal ability to push forward, but a supernatural strength that's found in God. He does ask us to take the steps of faith and use the strength that we have. "Go in the strength that you have" (Judges 6:14), and that's when we get to experience His supernatural strength when ours goes out.

I can just see the heads begin to turn as Paul walks back into the city. "Is that… no…. Surely not… is that, Paul? The guy we killed?" You better believe it was, and they messed with the wrong dude! Paul wasn't back for vengeance in a fleshly manner where he called each of the men to a fair one-on-one fight at city hall (though this would have been epic). Instead, he humbly goes about his business and prepares for where the Holy Spirit would lead him next. This is the ultimate slap in the face to his accusers. They beat him so badly to the point of near death, yet he kept preaching the Good News of Jesus.

I don't know about you, but if I was someone who watched this happen, I would want to follow him. If someone is willing to stay that committed to someone who isn't physically here on the Earth anymore, there must be something else going on inside Paul's heart, and we know there was. We all have our limits, we all have a breaking point, even the most trained soldiers in the world have breaking points, but not those who've been assigned to a task by the Holy Spirit. Almost all the early disciples were murdered for their faith along with countless others since then, yet people kept fighting until the very end and stayed committed to the preaching and ministry of Jesus. This is what "fighting the good fight of faith" looks like. When we live our lives passionately for Jesus, even when our circumstances aren't favorable, we keep going through the power of the Holy Spirit.

If you're like me, the fight mentality comes naturally, but if it's not sanctified by God, it becomes egotistical, and you will end up saying or doing things that aren't of God. After God radically changed my life, I was full of faith and full of fight, but I needed the family of God to come alongside of me and help me grow and mature in my faith.

I've seen many well-intended Christians (normally newly saved) be excited to fight for God, but they don't have the spiritual maturity yet to know how to go about this properly. They can begin to think that they see things that no one else sees and can become cynical but cover it up with spiritual talk, but really, it's rooted in pride. We must remember that Satan and his army are much more powerful than us by ourselves, and just because we have the Holy Spirit in us doesn't mean that everything we say and do is of God. If we aren't in step with the Spirit, we might find ourselves falling into the enemy's trap without even knowing it.

Look no further than the story of Samson (Judges 16). His strength was from his hair, but it was given to him by God. It became an idol, and he ended up dying because of his strength. I know that it was the temptation of Delilah that got him to reveal his secret, but he thought that he could continue to kill his enemies because of his strength, but God removed the strength from him once it was told. If we don't steward the strength that God gives us, it can be our downfall.

This isn't to discourage the new believer in their faith, in fact, we need more people on fire for God! Rather, it's a caution to continue to stay humble and gentle, but also remain stronger and use your fighter spirit for good. On the other hand, the seasoned believers need to welcome those who are on fire and let their fire continue to burn by having people like this around us. I've seen too many seasoned Christians miss out on a move of God because they were too threatened by the newly spirit-filled believers, and this is a sad thing. We all need each other, and we need to remind ourselves who the enemy is, and who it isn't.

Others of you might feel the exact opposite of Paul and find the "fight" mentality doesn't come easily. If that's you, that's okay, you're not alone! Unlike Samson, Gideon was not a warrior in the world's eyes or even his own. The nation of Israel was under attack and Gideon was hiding at the bottom of a winepress from his enemies when an angel appeared to him and called him "mighty warrior" (Judges 6:12). This was not sarcasm (or a typo), it was a prophetic word about how God was about to use him. He had no background in war like David, and he was as green as they come when it came to warfare. However, after throwing out a fleece to God to ensure He heard God correctly, he decided that God's words were enough to fight his enemy.

God powerfully used Gideon to accomplish more than he could have ever done on his own, and it's a great reminder for us today. If God calls you to it, He will equip you for it, and bring you through it. I'm not sure what your "winepress" is, but maybe God is calling you out from the safe zone into the faith zone, and this is where we watch God do the "immeasurably more" (Ephesians 3:20). Quit telling yourself that you can't do things and focus on what God can do. This is when we experience a supernatural fight that arises within us that only comes from God Himself.

No matter if you're like David, acted like Samson at times, or Gideon, God is still calling us to fight in His spiritual war. You win by not quitting once you've gotten knocked down. You don't have to be the strongest or toughest, you just need to not quit. This is what it means to have spiritual grit, to keep going when you're against the ropes in life. I believe if you keep trusting in God, He will bring you through the fight and you'll be victorious, and you will look back and see you've developed grit you never thought was possible.

Get back up and keep FIGHTING!

THE FINAL FIGHT

Jesus knew all throughout His ministry even when people were praising Him and when He was casting out evil spirits, that His real fight was coming. Every time He cast out an evil spirit, He was reminded why He came, and that was to defeat darkness. He knew He was going to take a blow from the enemy, but he also knew He would get back off that "mat" (death) and rise again and conquer His enemy and be victorious! (Revelation 1:18). The enemy thought he won after deceiving Adam and Eve in the garden, but God immediately put a curse on him and predicted his ultimate defeat.

"15 And I will cause hostility between you and the woman, and between your offspring and her offspring. He will strike your head, and you will strike his heel" (Genesis 3:15 NLT).

Bible scholar David Guzik writes:

"There is no doubt this is a prophecy of Jesus' ultimate defeat of Satan. God announced that Satan would wound the Messiah (you shall bruise His heel), but the Messiah would crush Satan with a mortal wound (He shall bruise your head). It was as if God could not wait to announce His plan of salvation, to bring deliverance through the one known as the Seed of the woman."[19]

Jesus' death and resurrection is the ultimate victory over Satan, and after all the time that had passed, his defeat came unexpectedly.

This is why Satan fights so hard against Christians because it's an extension of Jesus and he hates being reminded that he's been defeated. Jesus has already won the war, we are now in the in-between battle, and Jesus is building His church (His army) by bringing restoration back to the Earth like

God originally intended. At the same time, Satan knows that he's defeated and knows that he will one day be defeated forever (Revelation 20), and have no more power, so in the meantime, he does whatever he can to take as many people with him as possible. The only reason Jesus hasn't come back yet is because He's giving people the time to repent so that way, they aren't separated from Him for all of eternity (2 Peter 3:9). No matter what, we will either die and go be in Jesus' presence (which is still sharing in victory!), or He will come to get His church at the rapture (1 Thessalonians 4:13–18), and allow us to share in Jesus' victory by being in His presence away from the darkness of the world. Victory is ours for those who are in Christ!

You might feel like your back is against the ropes in this spiritual fight, but I can assure you that if you continue to press forward, you can have victory just as Jesus had victory. We share in His victory because His death covered the debt of our sins. If you feel like God hates you and is done with you, it's because you're not looking through the lens of victory, but rather defeat. We are not defeated, but rather conquerors. "Overwhelming victory is ours through Christ, who loved us" (Romans 8:37). If you're ready to throw in the towel and give up on your spiritual fight, I urge you to remind yourself, as well as the enemy, that you are on the winning side, not the losing side.

Paul knew this and spoke of it often. "But thank God! He gives us victory over sin and death through our Lord Jesus Christ" (1 Corinthians 15:57 NLT).

We share in Christ's victory; therefore, we can be victorious over the attacks of the enemy, and if you fall, just remember you are still victorious because you are on God's side. Keep growing stronger in your faith and continue to be more like Him and remember, one day we will reach the end of our fight when we are at home with The Lord, and we will be so thankful that we fought like we did!

We're fighting a fight that's already been won! We are victorious in Christ!

Do you have FIGHT when you're against the ropes?

CLOSING: SCORECARD

In every professional fighting match, the two fighters will gather in the center of the ring with their corners and wait for the ring judge to announce the official results from the judge's scorecards. These judges have been "keeping score" of the fight throughout the entire match and based on their evaluation of the fighters, the fighter who had the overall best score of the two wins the fight. Sometimes this is an easy process due to a knockout or an overwhelmingly one-sided fight. However, there are other times when this is a very intense moment because there's a very close fight. Throughout the years, there have been countless controversial decisions made by the judges, leaving the fighter who lost in shock. In fact, there have been times that people have suggested the fighter was completely robbed.

I'm so thankful that our spiritual fight isn't like this process; however, many people think that God (our judge) is tallying up our good deeds and subtracting our sins from them, lowering our final score. This is not at all what God does! We are saved and forgiven through our faith in Jesus and by the sacrifice of His blood. When we accept Him in our hearts, we are forever on His team as long as we genuinely have repented and followed Him and stayed committed to Him.

Our sins don't disqualify us like a fighter who does something to be "DQ'd." On judgment day, we can stand in the "middle of the ring" with Jesus and He will raise our hands up in victory over our opponent, Satan, and all of Heaven will applaud! I'm not sure what exactly this will look like, but perhaps those who we've "trained" with will also be standing by us to celebrate this eternal victory.

I like to think that all of the spiritual giants throughout the course of history will be around the "ring," nodding their heads in approval, and giving us a thumbs up knowing we kept the faith just as they did. While our names won't be written in the Bible, they will be written in the "Lamb Book of Life" which is our eternal reminder that we fought until the end. Maybe there are days in Heaven when we can go look at the book and see all the names in there and see those who impacted us along the way, as well as those we've impacted. Better yet, we will see them ourselves! (1 Corinthians 13:12).

This is the day that we look forward to, and we must stay focused and committed to the spiritual fight in the meantime. The grit that you develop in your spiritual fight can give others the grit they need to keep fighting theirs! We will never know the impact of our obedience until Heaven, but we can imagine the eternal impact of our disobedience both for ourselves and others. We will have our final judgment along with everyone else, and we want to show up knowing we gave it our all, nothing held back, not perfect (far from it actually), but we were committed to not giving up, and along the way, we discovered that God gave us the ability to do things we couldn't ourselves.

So, the next time your back is AGAINST THE ROPES, keep on fighting, and know you will be victorious when you have FAITH, FAMILY, and FIGHT!

BORN TO FIGHT

"He should be in the ring fighting."

These were the words that my dad told one of my friends at my wedding. I wasn't sure if either of my parents would show up for this milestone or not, but to my surprise, they were both there. My dad slipped in right before it started and sat next to my friend (Jason) who he recognized. My dad knew Jason because Jason's dad was my dad's boxing trainer back in the day.

As my dad watched me on my "big day," he looked at me on the stage and thought about how I needed to be in a boxing ring. It wasn't that my dad wasn't proud of me, but he couldn't understand why my life looked the way it did. I was raised for many years to fight, and I'm sure he always thought I would follow in his footsteps, and at one point, I thought the same thing. He couldn't imagine that his kid would be a preacher.

Jason, who watched my dad train over the years with his dad, knew where my dad was coming from because he grew up in a boxing home and his dad also has a fighter mentality; however, Jason responded and said, "He is fighting, he's just fighting a different fight."

SUMMARY

Against The Ropes: When a fighter is pinned against the ropes and has little room to escape.

Grit: "courage and determination despite difficulty." Throughout this book, we have looked at the ongoing battle of spiritual warfare (good vs evil), and we have looked at how we can use Faith, Family, and Fight against our spiritual enemy. For some, faith comes easier, for others, the family aspect is more natural, and for others, it's fighting. None of them are supreme over the others, and if we don't have them all, then we won't win when we're against the ropes. I want to recap what's been covered to make sure you are sent out in your fight with a good understanding of how to develop the spiritual grit you need to win.

First, You Must Have Faith: You must decide to put your FAITH in God when trials come your way, or you will never develop the GRIT you need to stay faithful to Him. Your faith is going to get tested, but we know that God will strengthen us in the midst of the test. We all put faith in someone or something, but God is the only one who will never fail us. You might have times when you've found yourself (or currently find yourself) putting your faith in someone or something, but God is the only one who will never fail us. Everyone finds themselves not being faithful to Jesus at times, but we shouldn't give up, rather let this build us up and become stronger in our commitment to Jesus. Once you've failed, keep putting your faith in Jesus. We have to develop a grown-up faith by trusting in God's plans, no matter how difficult they may be. God will use trials to refine our faith and help us learn to be grateful and humble in every situation. We need God-sized faith in order to see God-sized miracles.

Second, You Must Have Family: It is impossible to fight the spiritual fight alone. You need FAMILY because It's much easier to develop spiritual GRIT when you have them by your side! We all have family bonds, and we need to realize that family is a gift from God. We also must realize that families fight with one another. When this happens, we must learn to navigate through this and know who our enemy is and who it isn't.

Family isn't just blood, but also spiritual. Those who are children of God are the family of God. God puts spiritual family around us to help us grow in our spiritual grit.

When we follow God, we will need to choose to pursue the things of Him more than the things of the world. This includes severing some relationships with friends that prevent us from growing in our faith. We still love them, but we know the enemy can use this against us. When we find ourselves in a low place, it's important to have friends (family) that help us go through them.

We need to cheer on the family of God around us and help them grow into who they are called to be. We need to build them up, not tear them down. Our families should be the greatest source of encouragement in the spiritual fight, and we need to make sure to pave the way for future generations.

Third, You Must Have Fight: As your spiritual GRIT is developed, you must decide whether to continue to FIGHT or give up in the spiritual fight.

God places dreams inside each of us, and we need to fight for those God-given dreams.

When we experience failure, we must continue to fight through it. This is how we develop spiritual grit. We need to fight for greatness, not greatness by the world's standards, but by God's. We need to give God our all in everything we do. There are amazing women and men of God who displayed the warrior spirit in the Bible, and we too can share the same thing. We are warriors, we just must engage in the spiritual war to discover it. We were created with a fighting spirit.

If we're not careful, we'll end up fighting things we weren't meant to fight, and we need to use our energy fighting the good fight of faith. God didn't create us just to go through the spiritual motions, He created us to actually fight. We need to get to fighting!

The spiritual fight isn't a game, it's real. If we don't take the enemy seriously then we will certainly lose. The greatest opponent we will ever face isn't the enemy, it's ourselves. Our sinful nature (flesh) wants to do the opposite of what God wants, so we must fight it!

No matter how hard the fight might be, don't throw in the towel. Keep fighting, and God will give you the strength you need.

In the end, we know we will be victorious because we will stand with Jesus on judgment day, and He will reward us for all of eternity!

REFERENCES

1. Bill Welch, "Build Spiritual Resilience," Life, Hope & Truth, 12 May 2022, https://lifehopeandtruth.com/life/blog/build-spiritual-resilience/.

2. "On The Ropes," Sports Lingo, www.sportslingo.com/sports-glossary/o/on-the-ropes/.

3. "Boxing, Corner Men ," World of Sports Science, Encyclopedia.com, 18 Mar. 2024, https://www.encyclopedia.com/sports/sports-fitness-recreation-and-leisure-magazines/boxing-corner-men.

4. Kevin Mitchell,"Rumble in the Jungle: the night Ali became King of the World again," The Guardian, 29 October 2014, https://www.theguardian.com/sport/2014/oct/29/rumble-in-the-jungle-muhammad-ali-george-foreman-book-extract.

5. Wikipedia, s.v. "Rope-a-dope." 3 Dec. 2023, https://en.wikipedia.org/wiki/Rope-a-dope.

6. How Many Hours Does the Average Person Work Per Week?" Fresh Books, 17 Apr. 2023, https://www.freshbooks.com/hub/productivity/how-many-hours-does-the-average-person-work#:~:text=It%20has%20been%20estmated%20that,at%20work%20over%20your%20lifetime.

7. "What is cultural Christianity?" GotQuestions.org, https://www.gotquestions.org/cultural-Christianity.html.

8. Charles Gilman, HOW OFTEN DO DOCTORS GET A DIAGNOSIS WRONG?" Gilman & Bedigian, 25 Apr. 2023, www.gilmanbedigian.com/how-often-do-doctors-get-a-diagnosis-wrong/.

9. ESV Study Bible, Crossway Books, 2008.

10. David Busic, *Way, Truth, Life: Discipleship As a Journey of Grace.* (The Foundry Publishing, 2021).

11. Ryan Burge, "The Nones," Ryan Burge.Net, 29 Aug. 2017, https://www.drburge.com/books.

12. Tom Ward, "The Amazing Story Of The Making Of 'Rocky'," Forbes, 29 Aug. 2017, www.forbes.com/sites/tomward/2017/08/29/the-amazing-story-of-the-making-of-rocky/?sh=153cd235560b.

13. "Generation Z: 'The Loneliest, Least Resilient Demographic Alive' The Nones," SHRM, 17 Nov. 2023, www.shrm.org/topics-tools/news/inclusion-equity-diversity/the-least-resilient-demographic-alive.

14. "Michael Jordan On Being Cut From High School Varsity: 'I Just Wasn't Good Enough,'" Oldskoolbball, 7 Apr. 202, https://oldskoolbball.com/michael-jordan-high-school-varsity/.

15. "Dictionary.com | Meanings and Definitions of English Words," Dictionary.com, 17 Sept. 2020, www.dictionary.com/browse/greatness.

16. Wikipedia, s.v. "Ivan Drago," 19 Mar. 2024.

17. Subby Szterszky, "The Olympic Games: Perishable Wreaths, Gold Medals and True Identity," Focus On The Family Canada, www.focusonthefamily.ca/content/the-olympic-games-perishable-wreaths-gold-medals-and-true-identity.

18. "Shadowbox." Merriam-Webster Dictionary, www.merriam-webster.com/dictionary/shadowbox.

19. "Genesis 3 – Man's Temptation and Fall," Enduring Word, 8 Nov. 2023, enduringword.com/bible-commentary/genesis-3.